GHOSTS OF PENN'S WOODS

By Jeffrey R. Frazier

Author of *Pennsylvania Fireside Tales - Volumes 1 through 7*

It is said that the Spirits of buried men
Oft come to this wicked world again;
That the churchyard turf is often trod
By the unlaid tenants of tomb and sod,
That the midnight sea itself is swept,
By those who have long beneath it slept.
And they say of this old, mossy wood,
Whose hoary trunks have for ages stood,
That every knoll and dim-lit glade
Is haunted at night by its restless shade.

The Haunted Wood by Isaac McLellan (1806-1899)

Ghosts of Penn's Woods
By Jeffrey R. Frazier

Those who hike around the Loop Trail at Bear Meadows Natural Area near Boalsburg in Centre County may not see any ghosts there, but they may see this natural gargoyle, which, when we spotted it in 2007, provided a touch of the paranormal to this unusual spot.

Copyright 2011 by Jeffrey R. Frazier
Egg Hill Publications
113 Cottontail Lane
Centre Hall, Pa. 16828

Printed in the United States of America
Jostens Commercial Publications
401 Science Park Road
State College, Pa. 16803

All photos by the author, unless otherwise noted.

All rights reserved. No parts of this book may be used or reproduced without the express written consent of the author, except in the case of brief quotations included in critical essays and reviews.

ISBN 978-0-9652351-9-8

Cover: Ghostly orbs along Slippery Rock Gorge Trail near McConnells Mill State Park in Lawrence County (see Chapter 3 for more details about the spirits who make this woebegone spot their home).

GHOSTS OF PENN'S WOODS
(Table of Contents)

I.   Ricketts Glen State Park 1 ➔ pages 1 - 6

II.   Ricketts Glen State Park 2 ➔ pages 7 - 14

III.   McConnells Mill State Park ➔ pages 15 - 24

IV.   Fort Roberdeau State Historic Site ➔ pages 25 - 34

V.   Trough Creek State Park ➔ pages 35 - 44

VI.   Hickory Run State Park ➔ pages 45 - 52

VII.   R. B. Winter State Park ➔ pages 53 - 60

VIII.   Worlds End State Park ➔ pages 61 - 68

IX.   Gettysburg National Military Park 1 ➔ pages 69 - 74

X.   Gettysburg National Military Park 2 ➔ pages 75 - 84

XI.   Scotia Barrens ➔ pages 85 - 94

XII.   Leonard Harrison State Park ➔ pages 95 - 100

XIII.   Poe Valley State Park 1 ➔ pages 101 - 108

XIV.   Poe Valley State Park 2 ➔ pages 109 - 114

XV.   Hairy Johns ➔ pages 115 - 122

XVI.   Cornwall Furnace ➔ pages 123 - 134

INTRODUCTION

For those who may not remember or not know, the name Pennsylvania was bestowed upon the state by King Charles II of England when he granted the land to William Penn in 1681. Quaker Penn, in modest fashion, had suggested that his province be simply named *Sylvania,* meaning "Woodland", but the king wanted to honor Penn's father, an admiral in the British navy, and so the name chosen was Pennsylvania, or "Penn's Woods". The name was appropriate then because the state at that time was a vast woodland, and it seems appropriate that the same name is used as part of the title for this volume since the stories it contains are from those parts of the state that have been preserved as throwbacks to the time of William Penn and that period when the woods could still be found in their ancient state.

As my wife likes to say, "It's not hard to fall in love with the woods", and we both agree that that's particularly true in the fall of the year. When autumn comes it can inspire us with its beauty, but it can also sadden us. Because it's then that whiffs of dried leaves and dying plants serve as melancholy reminders of the passing of yet another year, and as the winds stir them their rustlings also cause us to pause and listen. To some it's the "pause that refreshes", just another way of enjoying nature, but to others the sounds might stimulate other thoughts; ideas that the soft chatter is something almost supernatural, and that, if we are even more attentive and observe even more carefully, we might actually see the passing of a ghost.

Why is it that the dark shadows of the deep woods seem to draw us to them? Is it a vague notion that they hold secrets that we must discover, a deep-seated need to find those who can tell us their little-remembered tales, or do the ghosts they harbor whisper to us in an attempt to draw us in and keep them company? There are those who would say that the latter is true; that there are ghosts in Penn's Woods; images of air that are lonely, remorseful, and on an endless quest. In fact, during the forty plus years I've spent collecting Pennsylvania's legends and folktales (see www.pafiresidetales.com) many people have asked me if I believe in ghosts myself.

My personal opinion is that the phenomenon is a real one, but the tales that follow are not meant to persuade anyone as to whether ghosts have supernatural origins or are artifacts of something that does not transcend the laws of nature at all; something explainable that is a part of nature that remains hidden to us. I do believe, however, that the encounters recorded in this book will go a long way toward persuading some that ghosts are not just figments of certain gullible individuals' imaginations. In fact I would go so far as to say that the individuals who told me their stories would all serve as reliable jurists in any court of law; none would be classed as heavy drinkers, drug users, or compulsive liars.

The approach used to compile the stories was three-fold. First the tales needed to be centered in or around Pennsylvania's state parks and historic sites in order to create an interest in and an appreciation for the natural and historic treasures Pennsylvania has to offer, particularly since Pennsylvania's State Park system was named the National Gold Medal Award Winner as best in the country for 2009-2011. Secondly I wanted the tales to be "first-hand" accounts; that is, heard directly from those who experienced the chilling events themselves rather than secondhand accounts handed down to my sources by others. Thirdly, if first-hand sources could not be found I then wanted to see if I could obtain a photo of the ghost site which manifested the phenomenon known to ghost hunters as "orbs".

There are those who think the circular white objects that sometimes unexpectedly appear in digital photos, especially those taken at night or in dimly lit circumstances where a flash is needed to illuminate the object being photographed, are spirit manifestations, or actual physical evidence of ghosts who wish to make their presence known to us. But to those who have studied the phenomena scientifically the "orbs", as they are often referred to, do have a more mundane explanation. To these experts the white balls of light are nothing more than reflections, or "backscatter", off foreign particles like dust, pollen, water droplets, or other similar objects, on or behind the camera lens.

Nonetheless, these mysterious spheres do cause us to ponder them when they appear in photos of supposedly haunted spots, and so there will always be those who prefer to think of them as having otherworldly origins. Readers of the following pages who hope to see such photos will not be disappointed since there are a number of these types of pictures. But it's the stories themselves that might hold an even greater appeal to those who wish to become further acquainted with Pennsylvania's ghosts and ghostly lore. May your armchair journey be filled with happy hauntings.

GHOSTS OF PENN'S WOODS

RICKETTS GLEN STATE PARK 1

Visitors to Ricketts Glen State Park in Luzerne, Sullivan, and Columbia Counties are most likely drawn here by its scenic waterfalls, and there's no doubt that the publicity is well-deserved and accurate. The hike along the Falls Trail will afford the adventurous with views of twenty-one impressive mini-Niagaras whose cascading heights range from 11-feet to 94-feet, but the trek is not for the faint-of-heart. It is a strenuous ramble that can only be accomplished by walking along slippery trails that are not only narrow but also remarkable for their vertigo-inducing drop-offs to the rushing waters of Kitchen Creek below. The scenes through the gloomy mists of Glens Natural Area, with its trees that are said to be as old as five-hundred years, evoke images of some spirit-haunted forest or of a woods straight out of *Grimm's Fairy Tales* from which Trolls, Gnomes, or even Hansel and Gretel's wicked witch might emerge at any moment. Of course no such encounters like this have ever been reported here, but the Glens does have its ghosts. At least that's what the old-timers in the area used to claim, and there are those yet today who will swear that not only is the old story a true one, but that the ghosts of which it tells still haunt the shore line and waters of the park's Lake Jean.

Long-time residents of the area are fond of recalling that the resident ghosts of the Glens make their home at the tip of a

GHOSTS OF PENN'S WOODS

small Glens' peninsula that stretches out into Lake Jean, near the Visitors Center. On this Outer Camping Loop, as it's called today, there is an amphitheatre as well as sites for campers, but back in the mid-1800's, when Lake Jean was known as Mud Pond, there was only a log cabin sitting on this same site. The old place was not a chalet; it afforded only the most meager shelter to the German family that decided to homestead here many decades before Colonel R. B. Ricketts' began to buy thousands of acres of land in the area to further his business interests.

The Getz's, as the family was called, managed to eke out a subsistence living by gardening, farming, and killing the wild game that abounded in the surrounding virgin forest. They did not have a large family, but they did have a small boy who was the "apple of their eye". They would do anything to make him happy, and that's why when he asked for a pair of ice skates for Christmas one year they didn't hesitate in granting his wishes. That Christmas Eve proved to be a special one for the nine-year-old, who was delighted to get the gift he had so earnestly desired. But his joy was short lived when his parents warned him that the water on the nearby pond had not yet frozen solid, and therefore was still too dangerous for him to try out this new skates.   His look of disappointment must have affected his parents' happiness as well, but they all went to bed contented with the prospects of enjoying their new presents on the following day.

GHOSTS OF PENN'S WOODS

The parents fell asleep quickly, but the young man kept thinking of his new silver skates, and he had to have one more look. Quietly as he could, he got out of bed and tip-toed to the Christmas tree in the corner of the cabin. Soon he was holding his new skates in his hands, and as he looked at them the allure of the pond outside proved to be overwhelming. In a moment he was at the waters' edge, and then the skates were on his feet and he was skimming over the ice. The experience proved to be as exhilarating as he had imagined, but as he skated closer and closer to the middle of the pond, he began to hear the sounds of cracking ice. Then, without so much as any further warning, the ice gave way and he was sinking deeper and deeper into the frigid waters. The icy water was numbing, but he managed to muster enough strength to scream for help anyway, and his distraught cries awakened his parents. Immediately they realized what had happened, and they both rushed to the rescue. However, in their haste they lost all sense of caution, and they too soon found themselves drowning in the ice-cold waters of Mud Pond.

It wasn't until several days later that passersby noticed the seemingly-deserted homestead. Their concerns led to the discovery of three sets of footprints in the snow, all of which led from the cabin to the nearby pond. Then when they saw the holes in the ice their worst fears were realized. After that time no one wanted to come near the place since it was thought that the former inhabitants' ghosts were haunting the site. Rumors of disembodied voices and screams, and reports of strange

GHOSTS OF PENN'S WOODS

lights emanating from under the lake surface kept people away, and soon the cottage fell into disrepair. But the inhospitable-looking abode eventually was discovered by hunters and fisherman who were either not aware of its haunted reputation of were not intimidated by it, and they began to use it for temporary shelter during their hunting and fishing trips into the area. The overnighters' stays in the old place seemed to set well with the ghosts, because none of the short-term guests were ever said to have been scared away. But there were reportedly several unsettling episodes that, once their stories became widespread, could have deterred some of those visitors from seeking shelter there again.

One of these ghostly encounters occurred on a cold autumn night during hunting season in an unknown year when a lone hunter found himself caught in the woods as darkness began to fall. He knew of the deserted Getz place near the pond in the forest, and so he headed there in hopes of at least having some shelter for his nighttime stay in the wilds. After entering the cabin he noticed that the glass in one of the windows had been partially broken out, and so he looked for something he could use to cover it and thereby make the place a little less drafty. Finding nothing that would serve his purpose, the man gave up and went to bed. Then sometime in the middle of the night he was awakened by a sound like branches scraping on the outside of the wall where the broken window was located. He was too tired and sleepy to look into the matter at that moment, but when he looked over at the window the next morning he was surprised to see that the windowpane had been repaired. Those who heard the story from the man would later say that he swore he would never stay there again.

Similar stories soon surfaced as well. One told of a group of hunters who decided to spend a night in the cabin during a weekend hunting expedition. Just as they were going to bed they claimed they heard "foreign" voices outside, but when they went to investigate they could see no one around. However, much to their amazement, the next morning they found that sometime in the middle of the night the dirty supper dishes they had left unwashed the night before had been washed by silent unseen hands. Later on other hunters and fishermen who stayed there would report similar events and relate that whenever they moved something in the cabin they would find it back in its original spot in the morning. Eventually, however, the old place fell into a state of total disrepair and it was torn down. That, so thought the locals, would end the hauntings as well. But it turns out they were wrong.

To this day the encounters still occur. In the summer of 2008, for example, a camper at the haunted spot on the park's Outer Camping Loop came into the park office one morning to complain that he had been awakened by strange "foreign-sounding" voices outside his tent the night before and that one of those people had slapped his tent with their hand. However, the most unsettling part had been that when he rushed outside to see who it was, he saw no one around no matter in which direction or how far he looked. Then too there are those who say that fishermen have reported that when fishing out on Lake Jean at night, they sometimes notice a soft yellow underwater glow that appears in the middle of the lake. It is said that whenever they row out to investigate, the eerie luminescence disappears, but there are reports that also claim that when these same fishermen peer down into the water they are horrified to see three faces staring back at them from what was thought at one time to be the watery Christmas Eve grave of the family who once lived here.

View of the haunted Outer Camping Loop and the surface of Lake Jean where the faces appear

RICKETTS GLEN STATE PARK 2

Although Ricketts Glen State Park has its own ghosts, visitors who wish to search for other spirits in the area may want to visit the nearby ghost town of Ricketts. It is believed to be the refuge of many ghosts, and there are those who have heard them milling about and murmuring to one another as though they are confused and are trying to decide what they need to do to break the bonds of this world and pass on to the next. Just like the park, the little town was named for Robert Bruce Ricketts, who enlisted in the Pennsylvania Light Artillery as a private at the outbreak of the Civil War in 1861 and distinguished himself as an artillery officer later in the war. His valorous service, including his battery's defense of Cemetery Hill on the second day's Battle of Gettysburg in 1863, led to his advancement through the ranks until he achieved the rank of Colonel. After the war he was equally successful, eventually acquiring over 80,000 acres of land in Sullivan, Luzerne, and Columbia Counties to further his lumber interests. The small lumbering town that grew up here was named Ricketts in his honor, and by the early 1900's it had become a thriving community with a hotel, two schools, and several houses of worship. At its peak, the mountain town boasted upwards of 175 houses and had its own blacksmith, doctor, railroad station, and even a baseball team. But the lumber industry was the driving force behind the area's prosperity, and in addition to the town's stave mill and spool mill, there were several nearby lumber camps that provided employment as well.

GHOSTS OF PENN'S WOODS

It was an economic boom for local farmers who could sell their produce to the camp workers, many of whom were employed by the Trexler and Turrell Lumber Company. The men were a mixed breed of many nationalities, and it is said that in some camps you could not hear anyone speaking a word of English. Each camp had its own foreman, and some of them are remembered by locals yet today; men like Johnny Lane, who ran the camp near present-day Lake Jean, and who had the reputation of being as hard working as his men. Lane was also considered to be as "clean living" and "God-fearing" as they come. In fact one day, locals say, Lane heard one of his workers swearing and took it as a direct insult to the Almighty. The foreman wasn't swayed by the man's protests that his cursing hadn't been that bad and really hadn't even done the situation justice, and without hesitation fired him on the spot. It was probably a "hard pill" for the fired worker to swallow since it meant he would be losing his 15-cents-an-hour wages, but he probably did not miss the hazards of the job or its ten to twelve hour working day.

There are many reports in the historical record of the region that reveal just how common fatalities and horrific injuries could be in the lumber camps of Colonel Ricketts' era. The first recorded fatality near Ricketts, for example, occurred in May of 1891 when 24-year-old Frank Farrell was crushed by a large limb he was cutting off a maple tree. The list goes on and on, with the death of Lincoln Ross who fell from a railroad car at Ricketts in March of 1892; the accidental death of William Green who died from a horrible gash he received in June of 1892 when a limb he was cutting fell on his shoulder; and the demise of Michael Shay who died from a similar accident in January of 1893. But there is another account of an accidental death at Ricketts that may not have been preserved in the historical record. At least those who remember the tale do not remember the victim's name anymore today, and so the recollection may just be an orally-preserved record of the death of Frank Farrell, William Green, or Michael Shay. On the other hand, it's probable that the victim may have been somebody else entirely, and if so, it might explain why his spirit cannot find rest after all these years; cannot find peace until the account of his death is preserved in a more permanent way than having to rely upon word of mouth to do so.

Although this orally-preserved account is not specific about the year of the accident, nor about the names of the men involved, it is very specific in its other details. According to the tale, the fatality occurred at Ricketts, and since the Trexler and Turrell operation began to build the town in 1890, it's possible that the accident in question occurred at that time. In any case the victim is said to have been a relatively new lumberman, still on his first year on the job. His older brother, on the other hand, had been working there for some time, and, as a more experienced "woods hick" with a better understanding of the dangers of the job, had been assigned to work with his sibling to be sure he didn't get injured and got proper training. The two brothers made a good team, but at some point they may have gotten too self-confident; too wrapped up in their ability to fell more trees than anyone else in any given period of time. At least that may be one explanation as to what happened one day when the two men were sawing down a particularly large tree and misjudged the direction and rate of its fall. It's recalled that the tree came down so fast that the younger brother never had a chance to dodge it. He was crushed like an egg shell by the forest behemoth, and his death was instantaneous. Although his brother may have been left momentarily speechless at the horror he was witnessing, it's said that when he did recover his voice his screams of anguish could be heard by all the workers at the job site. And there are those who say that those same screams can be heard yet today if you are there at the right time and the ghosts decide you need to be reminded of the terrible tragedy that once occurred here.

The Trexler and Turrell lumbering operations at Ricketts continued until they cut the final tract of lumber off Cherry Ridge in the fall of 1913. By the end of the next year the town was nearly deserted, with only five families still living there. Eventually everyone moved away, and their houses collapsed or were torn down for their lumber, including the large hall once used as a meeting house for the Patriotic Order of the Sons of America lodge. Today, the only vestige of the town that remains along Route 487, four miles north of the park, is a large concrete bunker that was once part of the pump house for the town's fire station. It's near this pump house bunker that someone once planted a tree on the same spot where the younger brother was crushed to death while his older brother could only stand by and helplessly watch it happen. It may have been an attempt to memorialize the young man's fate, but, if so, it did not pacify his soul.

The tree is still there today, just where it was planted, but there is something odd about it. Although the tree sits on what should be hallowed ground it looks like it's been covered with a killing frost, which makes it appear as white as a ghost. The other thing that is notable about the tree is that nothing ever grows on it; no leaves, no fruit, no berries of any kind. Its bare branches represent a strange puzzle that tweaks the imaginations of ghost hunters and others who search for the mysterious and the extraordinary. In fact those who come here to see it for themselves have reported hearing moans and screams in the wind that sweeps through the trees in the forest near the pump house bunker. Then there are people who claim to have heard other strange sounds as they've walked through the ghost town, and they include a Ricketts Glen State Park staff member who experienced the sounds first-hand one afternoon after escorting a school group around the historic setting.

She had circled the town site with the children and their teachers, and had gotten everyone back to the pump house bunker when she heard faint voices in the wind. Surprised that she had left some individuals so far back, she listened again and decided the sounds were coming from the site of the town's general store, which was on the other side of the town. She immediately went to investigate, but once she got there she was more than a little shaken when she realized there was no one around. To this day she says she "still gets goose bumps just talking about it". However, maybe tales like this will keep the memory of the old town alive, and maybe that fact will at last give the ghost of the young lumberman some peace. Enough peace, perhaps, that it can finally move on to the next plane, leaving the site of its horrible death behind once and for all.

The old pump house at the ghost town of Ricketts

GHOSTS OF PENN'S WOODS

View of the "ghost tree" near the old pump house

GHOSTS OF PENN'S WOODS

Another view of the "ghost tree" after clouds blocked the sun and noticeably darkened the area (notice orb at lower right)

McCONNELLS MILL STATE PARK

Anyone looking for ghosts in this Lawrence County state park would probably think that a good place to start would be in the area called Hell's Hollow. The name certainly evokes thoughts of the paranormal, just as it did in earlier times when locals gave this stretch of the Slippery Rock Gorge its name; but the events that led to that intimidating title were not as appalling as we might imagine today. It turns out that geological rather than supernatural events provided the source for that designation, and evidence of those activities can be seen down in Hells Hollow yet today, and some say the same can be said of Its ghosts.

One of the unique things about this area is its surface layers of limestone; a geological oddity for western Pennsylvania. The easily-extracted rocks proved to be a boon for local entrepreneurs, who wanted to use the stones for making lime. As a result, there were many lime kilns built in the hollow, and the remains of one of them can still be seen near the impressive waterfall that was there in that day and which is worth the short hike down into the hollow to see today.

The lime making operations proved to be profitable enterprises, but the kilns gave the ravine a unique appearance. Dense smoke from their fires filled the hollow both night and day, and in the darkness those same fires lit up the clouds of smoke with an unearthly orange glow. The fiery hellhole led locals to decide that there was no better name for the place than that used to refer to the devil's abode, and the name caught on. It has clung to the spot ever since, just like some of the spirits that are said to cling to many other parts of this same gorge. And it is one of those areas that does at least have the appearance of being a more likely spot as a home for ghosts.

Hikers trekking down into the gorge via the opposite end of the Slippery Rock Gorge Trail may find that here they are just as apt to find their thoughts turning to things that are not of this world as they were when hiking down into Hells Hollow. Maybe that's because they start at the old mill, with its decidedly haunted appearance and history, but if not, then it's the trailside scenery that causes the mind to wander. Impressive rock formations line the banks of Slippery Rock Creek through here, and some of them look like strange gargoyles glaring down at passersby. But the utter darkness of this somber and lonely spot, where the sun never seems to shine even at midday, evokes strange feelings in people as well. Some will tell of the ever-present mists that rise from the small creek and the rivulets that feed it. The white columns of fog, which sometimes seem to dance and sway in the forest twilight, serve as reminders of any spirits that dwell here; create the impression that this is indeed a place where ghosts abide. And if that were not enough to convince anyone that they are in an other-worldly place, they need only notice the many roots that seem to be strangling the huge boulders which they've overgrown to the point that the entangled stems look like a mass of writhing snakes or the tentacles of some malevolent sea monster.

GHOSTS OF PENN'S WOODS

But are these surreal reminders really clues pointing to ghostly inhabitants or do they just cause us to think that way? Imaginations can run wild when stimulated by such things, and these same stimulants can be found in many spots in the Gorge. Locals, on the other hand, do state that there have been many people who have drowned in Slippery Rock Creek over the years; mostly the more adventurous types who did not exercise proper care when hiking along the slick banks of the stream, climbing the many rock ledges along its banks, or when swimming or boating in the same waters. Perhaps it is their spirits that haunt the place today and which appeared as orbs on the author's photos taken along the Slippery Rock Gorge Trail (see cover photo and photos at end of this story). But there are two ghosts in other parts of the park that have achieved more notoriety than any others that might still flit through the dark shadows of its loneliest spots; one from the days when the old mill was still in operation and the other from more modern times.

It is not known today whether the mill's supposed ghost originates from the time of original owner Daniel Kennedy or from the era of Thomas McConnell, the mill's second owner, but, according to the old tale, it was the massive equipment in the mill that caused the man's death. The unfortunate worker, whose name is no longer recalled, was a full time mill employee and lived close enough to the operation that he walked to work every morning and then back home in the dark every night; always along the same route and with his lunchbox in one hand and a lantern in the other. It was a good secure job, but it could be a dangerous one as well, as the man was to find out.

GHOSTS OF PENN'S WOODS

Regardless of whether the equipment needed repairs, or whether the mill-hand just got careless, the end result was that he was caught up in and crushed to death by the belts and grinding stones of the mill. It was said to have been a horrible and excruciating way to die, and, typical in such cases, it was thought that because of his terrible death, the man's spirit could not move on to the next world; or at least that's what local rumors seem to indicate.

Stories that have persisted for decades here say that on certain nights of the year after visitors have left the park and the only sounds are that of the night wind and the waters of the creek, a ghostly form makes its own visit to the mill. Those who have the ability to sense such things, and who have been brave enough to stay and watch, say that this vaporous image can be seen walking toward the old wooden building and then entering it. Once the apparition enters, so say these same observers, the interior is lit up with a lantern-like glow and anguished screams inside the mill pierce the shroud of darkness like a knife. There is usually no one there to hear the awful cries, except perhaps other spirits that might be listening nearby.

There is one more ghost that haunts the park, or at least that's what locals say, and this "image of air" can be found, summoned would be a better word, at the quaint covered bridge that spans the creek near the mill. According to the popular account that seems to travel from place to place and appears to be nothing more than a modern-day urban legend, the young lady whose spirit haunts the bridge was killed there in an auto accident sometime in the first half of the twentieth century. Still confused, the girl's lonely spirit is said to appear to those who park their car on the bridge at midnight, turn off the car's lights, and honk the car's horn three times. If this is done, it's believed by some, the spiritual essences of the forlorn lady manage to materialize enough so that her image can be seen in the car's rear view mirror, but only for an instant. Anyone seeing the reflection will naturally turn around to get a closer look, but when they do so the ghost is no longer there; it has dissipated back into the misty darkness, perhaps to join the spirit that haunts the old mill that sits nearby.

The haunted mill

The haunted mill and its haunted covered bridge

Interior view of the haunted mill.

A view of Hell Run at Hells Hollow Falls

GHOSTS OF PENN'S WOODS

The ghostly orbs along Slippery Rock Gorge Trail

GHOSTS OF PENN'S WOODS

More ghostly orbs along Slippery Rock Gorge Trail

FORT ROBERDEAU

For those who wish to get a feeling of what it was like on the Pennsylvania frontier during the days of the Revolutionary War there's no better place to visit than the Fort Roberdeau Historic Site in Tyrone Township of Blair County, and no better time than a day of "Indian Summer" in the fall of the year. In fact those who spend a day here are almost guaranteed to achieve a heightened appreciation for the frontiersmen of that era. But there may be added bonuses too, including a closer communion with nature, seeing a fiery sunset as Old Sol sinks slowly in the western sky, and catching a fleeting glimpse of one of the fort's ghosts.

Built in 1778, the fort was constructed to protect lead mining operations in the beautiful Sinking Valley of, what was then, Bedford County. The lead was badly needed to make bullets for soldiers of the Continental Army, and General Daniel Roberdeau spear-headed the effort to find a source for that much-needed metal. When that source was found in Sinking Valley, Roberdeau not only paid a personal visit to the area to verify the authenticity of the claims, but, once he had done so, also decided that a fort was needed to afford some degree of protection for the miners who would be mining the ore.

The stockade was not built like most frontier forts of that time. Thick under-layments of limestone and a thin layer of topsoil precluded the normal methods of construction. Usually the wooden sides of a fort consisted of vertical posts that were set into deep trenches that were then back-filled with dirt. In

Fort Roberdeau's case, however, the number of vertical posts were necessarily minimized and used to hold horizontal timber walls in place instead. But the end result was impressive, and the replica of the fort that stands there today serves as a testimony to that fact. It must also have impressed and intimidated the British Rangers, Iroquois Indians, and local "loyalists" who may have thought about attacking the place; there is no record that they ever attempted to do so.

But the men of local militia units and ranging companies that manned the fort were well armed and ready for any such maneuvers. The many muzzle ports in the log walls afforded them an opportunity to spray attackers with withering fire from any angle, and the four "4-pounder" cannons at their disposal would have kept an invading force at bay as well. And in addition to those critical factors, the officers of the fort were experienced soldiers.

Commandant of the fort in 1778 was Major Robert Cluggage. Fresh from his service commanding Thompson's Rifle Battalion during the Siege of Boston in 1775, he had risen to the rank of Colonel in New York. As an outstanding patriot and accomplished leader, Cluggage knew how important the Fort Roberdeau site was to the cause of the fledgling nation, and perhaps it was him who even gave the place its nickname, the "Lead Mines Fort". But Major Cluggage's task was not an easy one. It may have seemed to him at times that troops came and went with the wind, given the fact that the average enlistment time for his militiamen was only 30 to 60 days. Nonetheless, he had a good officer corps, including men like his brother, Captain Thomas Cluggage, Captain John Lane, Captain John MacDonald, Captain Henry Black, and Lieutenant Robert Galbraith.

The men and officers of the fort were housed in log cabins built inside the stockade, with one of the units designated as the "Officers' Quarters". It served as the administrative office of the fort and the living quarters for its leaders. Today a replica of those same Officers' Quarters sits inside the fort, directly to the right as visitors walk through the main entrance. At first glance it appears to be like all the other cabins in the fort, and it does not give any indication that it might be a haunted place. However, there are those who know otherwise; those who have personally seen the cabin's ghost and who are not afraid to talk about it.

Every year at the fort there is a French and Indian War celebration that draws re-enactors from far and wide. Such was the case back in the spring of 1981 when six to eight of those same re-enactors were staying in the Officers' Quarters for the duration of the historic activity. The March weather was particularly cold that year, and the overnights in the log cabin were frigid ones. There were even late spring snowfalls at that time, and on some nights the howling winds whistled around the cabin and sent snowflakes through the larger gaps between the logs that formed the cabin's walls. The frigid weather prompted the men in the cabin to light a roaring fire in the building's fireplace so the interior temperature would be raised to a point where they could sleep more comfortably, but even with the fire going they found sleep was hard to come by.

They would drift off into a fitful slumber but would periodically be awakened by bone-chilling breezes that seemed to travel through the cabin. Anyone who awoke would look over at the fireplace to make sure the fire was still going, and if it was low they would get up to put more wood onto the dwindling blaze and then go back to bed. However on one night in particular it appeared to one re-enactor that something different was going on. Several times that evening the man had been jarred awake by drafts of super-chilled air, and each time he had looked over at the fireplace to check on the fire. Awakened once more he looked over at the fire again, but this time he saw one of the other re-enactors sitting on the fireplace hearth and leaning toward the crackling blaze. It was almost as though the man had decided to abandon his bunk altogether and trade it for the relative warmth of the flames.

The re-enactor appeared to be contentedly warming his hands. He was facing the fire with his arms stretched out toward it, and his hands were over the coals. Surprisingly, for this time of night, he appeared to be fully dressed in his re-enactor clothes, including his tri-cornered hat, bleached linen shirt with black collar, breeches, and blue army overcoat once typically worn by soldiers of the Continental Army. It was a bit confusing to the drowsy observer, and his first reaction was to ask the man on the bunk beside him where the re-enactor by the fireplace was going. When the man checked the other bunks and realized all were occupied, he sleepily replied that no one was going anywhere!

GHOSTS OF PENN'S WOODS

It was at that point that the figure got up and turned directly toward the men watching it. Then it turned again and began walking towards the only way out of the place. Whereas it had originally appeared to be as solid as a real person, it now seemed to fade into oblivion as it got closer to the exit, gradually becoming fainter and fainter until it disappeared altogether as it passed through the solid door. The full frontal view had not lasted long, but it was long enough that the transfixed observers noticed the apparition had a medallion of some sort hanging from a chain around its neck and the "facings' on its coat were yellow in color.

The next morning the two men related their experience to their comrades, and one of the re-enactors, who was more knowledgeable about Continental uniforms than the others, declared that the yellow decorative trim, or "facings", on the apparition's coat indicated that it was from a uniform of the Thirteenth Virginia Continental Line. It was a surprising statement given the fact that the forces that had manned the fort had never been Continental troops at all, but rather were ranger and militia units who, like other frontiersmen of the day, typically wore buckskin outfits rather than army uniforms. It was a puzzle that would go unsolved for many years, only being resolved by yet another bizarre event; one that would make it seem that the ghost in the Officers' Quarters had come to set history straight.

The men's description of the medal around apparition's neck would prove accurate enough that the ornament would later be identified as German in origin. However, questions about the origins of the ghost's uniform seemed destined to be unanswerable ones until one day, five years after their ghost sighting, the two men who had seen the apparition firsthand were driving along Blacksnake Road near Orbisonia in Huntingdon County. They had driven here on a tip that the Cluggage brothers, the rangers who had manned Fort Roberdeau, were buried near here, and almost as though they had been guided by unseen forces, the travelers were drawn to a weathered stone farmhouse that looked old enough be one of the original buildings in the valley.

    A loud knock on its heavy wooden door did not go unanswered long, and the young woman who opened it was not unfriendly. When asked if she knew anything about the burial places of rangers Thomas and Robert Cluggage, she surprised the inquirers with an invitation to come out back to an old family cemetery. Here, she said, was the final resting place of Robert and his son, who, she proudly proclaimed, were her ancestors. After escorting her guests over to see the sought-after tombstones the young lady began to talk about them. The conversation inspired her, and she excused herself, saying she wanted to get a family heirloom that she thought the men might enjoy seeing. With that she went back inside the impressive manor house that looked like it could hold ancient secrets of all manner and kind.

    It wasn't long afterwards that she came back out carrying a document that she said was an original letter written To Major Robert Cluggage by Richard Peters, permanent secretary of General George Washington's Board of War. The brief dispatch stated that Cluggage could give his rangers the Continental Line uniforms that had been delivered to him by "Lt. Col. Campbell of the 13th Virginia Regiment". It seemed to be the lost key; the final piece to the mystery about the ghost's uniform. If so, then maybe the ghost in the Officers' Quarters, knowing that the information it wished to share with others has been disseminated at last, has found the peace it must have been seeking all these years.

At least it would seem so, because one of the re-enactors who originally saw the wraith has tried to see it a second time, but to no avail. He has stayed in the cabin on the same date as that of his first encounter, and he has stayed there more than once on that same date. However, much to his disappointment, the specter has never paid him a visit again. On the other hand there are those who say that maybe the spirit has moved to another spot, and it may be the phantom which seems compelled to guard the fort even yet today. For there is another, more persistent and more well-known, ghost tale associated with this place, and local students were once drawn here to see the dark apparition for themselves. It is a ghost hunt best done at nighttime in the moonlight, according to their accounts, and, for those brave enough to attempt it, the final leg of the search should be done on foot.

That investigation starts when you turn off Township Road 574 onto the side road leading to the fort. The thoroughfare, now paved, passes through a field that is often planted in corn. About a half mile into the field the seeker should stop and look at the phone poles that stand alongside the road ahead. Here, pacing back and forth across the road, will sometimes be seen a dark figure which appears to be guarding the path back to the site of the reconstructed fortress. There have been some strange sensations experienced by those who walked up to the spot where they saw the black form, which disappeared as they approached it, but no harm has ever come to anyone who attempted such an encounter. Perhaps the spirits here are glad to have company once in a while, or maybe they are just satisfied with their surroundings, which serve as reminders of their thrilling days on the frontier.

Main entrance and side view of the fort

GHOSTS OF PENN'S WOODS

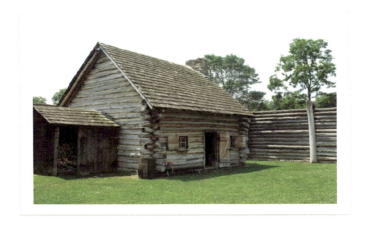

The Officers' Quarters and the fireplace inside where the ghost was seen by the re-enactors in 1981

GHOSTS OF PENN'S WOODS

View of the roadway leading to the fort and where the ghostly sentinel is sometimes seen.

TROUGH CREEK STATE PARK

Although not one of the largest of Pennsylvania's 117 state parks, the 554-acre Trough Creek State Park has many other attractions (worldly and other-worldly) to compensate for its smaller size. Among those sights is the picturesque gorge or "trough" that was created by Great Trough Creek as it wore its way through Terrace Mountain. Today the creek drains into manmade Lake Raystown near the village of Entriken, and that body of water has become a favorite "haunt" of tourists coming to the region. But what most of those lakeside visitors most likely do not realize, however, is that there is an actual haunted spot in the nearby Huntingdon County state park; one claimed by a ghost that, considering the tale that's told about it, must be filled with both remorse and despair.

There are a number of unique and scenic spots in the park that seem to draw the crowds to them. Among these oft-visited places of interest is the precariously-perched Balanced Rock that teeters on the edge of a cliff overlooking nearby Rothrock State Forest. Right beside the rocky elevation on which the huge cliffside boulder sits is the renowned Rainbow Falls with its misty multi-colored arcs of light formed when the sun shines fully upon it. Not too far from here can be found the Raven Rocks that were once home to flocks of ravens which nested in them. The rocky cliffs are said to have a curious history. Local lore claims that the cliffs' large black avian inhabitants actually were an inspiration for Edgar Allen Poe when he supposedly visited here in 1870. He was so impressed by the melancholic appearance of the place, and by the forlorn sounds of the ravens, that he was inspired to write one of his most famous poems, even titling it after the bird that spurred his imagination. At least that's the story.

Among the other unusual spots in the park is the famous Ice Mine; a naturally occurring "ice box" that bathes tourists with its wintry blasts of cold air, even in summertime. Then, too, there is the solitary and little-visited Paradise Cemetery, a melancholy and lonely spot perched on the hillside directly above the well-preserved remains of the original Paradise Furnace, the iron furnace built here in 1827 by Reuben Trexler. The short hike up to the burial ground is rewarded with pleasurable views of many waterfalls created by a small steam as it spills over the rocky creek bed and makes it way down the mountain to join Great Trough Creek below. Once there, visitors to the cemetery will also be intrigued by its unusual tombstone.

Some believe that the headstone, with its odd face and inscription, marks the grave of a local Indian "princess", while others say it is just that of an early white settler. Although there are doubts about who's buried in this particular grave, its occupant seems unmoved by the controversy; at least there have never been any reports of spirits that haunt this sun-dappled and tree-shaded resting place. On the other hand, there is a possibility that the ghost of one of its residents does haunt a spot nearby.

Probably among the most well-liked and sought-ought attractions in the park is the ironmaster's mansion, which sits near the old furnace. Constructed in the mid-1800's as the ironmaster's homestead, the old house was eventually renovated after the area became a state park, and Trough Creek Lodge, as it's called today, can now be rented for overnight stays. It is expensive to stay there, but despite the cost it is rarely unoccupied. Regardless of its many guests and its age, however, there've never been any reports that the mansion is haunted. On the other hand it would not be surprising if reports like that would surface someday, especially since the bridge over nearby Great Trough Creek is reported to be haunted by the ghost of a young woman who, when in human form, once lived in the old house.

According to some accounts, she was the daughter of the ironmaster who resided there with the rest of his family at a time prior to the furnace's closure in 1856. Today some think her name was Catherine, and others say it may have been Mary Ann, the name of the first ironmaster's daughter and the name he bestowed upon the furnace before it was renamed Paradise Furnace. However it really doesn't matter since the ghost keeps to itself anyway, only appearing to a select few, and then only at seemingly random times.

The story of the ironmaster's daughter begins at her birth, when her father pre-arranged her marriage. Presumably he wanted her to be well-connected and assured of a life of relative ease, and so he arrived at some sort of an agreement with one of his wealthy ironmaster friends that the man's son would marry his daughter when both came of age. It seemed like a good plan, except his daughter's life took her down a different path and her heart was stolen by another; a man who was not the wealthy scion her father desired for her, but someone of an entirely different class.

Near the massive iron furnace at that time was a foundry called Savage Forge, and one of the young workers here had caught the eye of the young lady, who by that time had decided her father's choice of her husband left much to be desired. Romance between the young man at Savage Forge and the young lady blossomed to the point where she knew she needed to tell her father about their decision to wed. But she was not prepared for his diatribe and his hurtful accusations of parental disrespect. Her fate seemed sealed and the seemingly hopeless situation left her despondent

Local versions of the tale say that her entreaties to her father to change his mind about the prearranged nuptials fell on deaf ears, and as the wedding day approached she became more depressed and felt her life was no longer worth living if she couldn't marry the man she truly loved. She tried to resign herself to her fate, even to the point of trying on her wedding dress on the night before her wedding day. However, when she looked in the mirror it became too much to bear and she sank deeper into her depression. Soon she could be seen leaving the mansion house and heading toward the old wooden bridge that spanned the creek nearby.

It was summertime, and it may have seemed like myriads of fireflies were illuminating the pathway down to the bridge, but what might have been a delightful display to most of us did not change the young lady's mood. Once on the well-worn beams of the bridge's floor, she walked over to one of its side rails and threw herself into the murky waters below. It's said that when she drowned in those same waters, she was still wearing her wedding dress. Although she did not survive her plunge, her story has survived, but only because it's believed that her spirit still lingers at this same spot; and at least one man will attest to it.

One night about thirty years ago one of the employees of the nearby Youth Forestry Camp #3 was crossing the sturdy steel bridge that now spans the stream at the spot where the young woman drowned herself. It had been a hot and humid day, but temperatures had fallen considerably after the sun went down, and now a heavy mist was blanketing the dark and uninviting waters. The car's headlights lit up the swaying clouds of fog with an unearthly light, but then the mists seemed to part, revealing a smaller white cloud floating just above the surface of the stream. It was a curious occurrence, but the situation got even stranger as the man watched the small cloud form itself into an image of a young woman in a white wedding dress. Then, just as quickly as it had appeared, it sank into the creek and was gone.

There have been no reports of anyone sighting the ghostly image at the bridge in recent years, and so the more romantically inclined might like to think that she has been reunited with her true love in the next world. But there is an unmistakable aura of sadness at this spot, particularly in late spring or early summer. It's then when the ghost flower can be found growing in the shaded glens nearby, and it's that time of year when warm summer breezes sound like soft voices whispering in the trees as they talk in hushed tones about the tragedy that once occurred here. It is neither the season nor the place where the faint-hearted will want to be when night comes and twinkling swarms of fireflies seem to say "follow us into the shadows, and we will light your way".

Paradise Furnace

GHOSTS OF PENN'S WOODS

Paradise Cemetery

GHOSTS OF PENN'S WOODS

The Indian princess tombstone at Paradise Cemetery

GHOSTS OF PENN'S WOODS

Trough Creek Lodge (home of the early ironmasters)

Two views of the haunted bridge.

HICKORY RUN STATE PARK

Only an hour's drive from the Allentown and Scranton/Wilkes-Barre metropolitan area, Hickory Run State Park in Carbon County is notable for its three Natural Areas, one of which is a registered national natural landmark. The three areas, Mud Run, Mud Swamp, and Boulder Field, offer a cool refuge on hot summer days, and their numerous hiking trails also provide lots of opportunities for exploration and exercise. But the parkland was not always the inviting place we find here today.

When the first white settlers entered this expanse in the late 1700's they found it to be a dark and intimidating spot; a region overgrown with dense forests of huge trees, and terrain made impassable by fetid swampland and seemingly-bottomless bogs. Moreover, the rocky soil here made it unfit for farming. The vastness was so distinctly uninviting, in fact, that those first pioneers must have thought it was a portal to the underworld; a place that could only be enjoyed by the souls of those who were making their journey from this plane of existence on to the next. At least the name they assigned to this plot of real estate would indicate as much. They called it "Shades of Death".

Although those same settlers did not pass down accounts of any ghosts that they may have seen here, their name for the locale would in later years prove to be an appropriate one as far as ghostly inhabitants go. For there is at least one specter that is believed to cling to this spot since losing its life over 160 years ago when it was in human form and living along the waters of Hickory Run. Her name was Elizabeth Gould, or "Lizzie" to her family and friends, and she is buried in the park.

Lizzie Gould's story begins in 1849 when she and her six siblings, along with their parents, Isaac and Susan, lived in a pioneer cabin along the waters of Hickory Run Creek and near a small lumbering community also named Hickory Run. Gould had lumbering interests in the area, and was owner of several water-powered saw mills he had constructed along the creek, including dams that were built to provide a dependable water source for powering the mills.

Mr. Gould was not the only lumber baron here. There were numerous saw mills and dams at different locations along the stream bank, but directly above the Gould cabin, on one of the foothills of the Pocono Mountains, there was another mill and dam, owned by a wealthy Philadelphian. Mr. Gould had pleaded with the man, even taking him to court, not to build the dam at that site since he knew it would prove to be unstable ground if it became oversaturated. But his pleas had fallen on deaf ears and the dam was constructed anyway. It was an accident waiting to happen, and the Gould homestead was situated directly along the path where the loosed waters of the dam would come if the dam failed to hold. Then, during the last week of October, 1849, heavy rains fell continuously, both by day and by night, swelling mill dams and creeks alike.

GHOSTS OF PENN'S WOODS

Isaac Gould was away on business at that time, knowing he could count on his mill hands to look out for his family's safety. But Mrs. Gould did not heed their warnings on the 29th that the big dam above them would not hold much longer. Since she did not want to leave without her husband, two of the hands volunteered to stay with them that night. Mrs. Gould still refused to leave when Lizzie, returning from an errand that same day, reported that people were saying that the dam was about to give way. The family went to bed, but Mrs. Gould slept fitfully, and then at 4:00 AM was awakened by a faint rumbling sound, which increased to a loud roar at the seconds ticked by. Then she finally realized the horrible import of the menacing noise; the dam had burst.

The floodwaters, on their headlong rush to the Lehigh River, hit before she could warn the others, and they struck with such force that the cabin was lifted off its foundation and spun around like a top before coming to rest 500 feet down the mountain. The roof of the place had fallen into the house, and on top of that were numerous logs that had been carried along by the torrent. It was a miracle that any of the Goulds survived, but all of them did; all except one.

Mrs. Gould and both the mill hands managed to rescue all the children, but they could not find Lizzie. As the disheveled and shivering survivors sat on a pile of wreckage and driftwood, Mrs. Gould pleaded with the mill hands to keep looking for her eleven-year-old daughter, claiming she could hear her calling to her. It took almost super-human efforts, but eventually the men found the missing girl. Her lifeless body was buried under the pile of driftwood on which the wreckage of the house now rested.

There were many other victims of the flood as well, including the wife and all four children of village blacksmith Jacob West. Another child of the Gould's, their baby Winfield, would later die from overexposure to the cold October air on that fateful Halloween night. Joanna Gould, one of the surviving daughters would subsequently write that her father, after arriving later that afternoon, wept bitterly as he held the lifeless body of Lizzie in his arms. It must have been almost too much to bear on that sad day when he buried her in a lonesome hillside grave.

The existence of the little cemetery where she is interred, which sits in a secluded woodland vale above the Gould's original cabin site, has not been widely publicized by park officials, who hope to keep the burial ground and its tombstones safe from vandalism. But it is a sheltered, almost-forgotten, sanctuary anyway; a little off the beaten path and typical of an old mountain burial spot. Due to its isolation, the cemetery's inhabitants are left relatively undisturbed, but that peace and quiet does not seem to have brought the same solace to Lizzie. It's now believed by some that when thick clouds of mist drift into the graveyard off of nearby Hickory Run or whenever heavy rains drench the area, Lizzie's ghost is awakened from its slumber time and time again.

So it appears, if the park's stories are accepted as having any factual basis, that there is no rest for poor Lizzie, even yet today. This is particularly true on days of unsettled weather when strong gusts sweep storm clouds across leaden grey skies and fitful shadows flit across the leafy brown carpet of the forest floor. It is on such days, it seems, that people are more apt to hear Elizabeth's plaintive voice calling for her mother, just as Mrs. Gould thought she was doing on the day of the flood. The blustery weather appears to disturb Lizzie's soul, and on nights following days like these there have been park rangers who, while working there late at night, have reported seeing Lizzie's ghost darting through the park's camp ground and around the old chapel that stands across from the park office. However, it is on October 30th that the little girl's ghost is most likely to appear.

On Halloween night, the anniversary date of her death, it's said that at midnight her spirit can be seen walking through the graveyard where she's buried. However, none of today's park rangers claim to have seen that image themselves; mainly because they say they do not have the courage to go there on that particular date and at that particular time. They have decided that they do not want to walk around among the nighttime shadows while autumn winds send dried leaves scattering and rattling around the weathered tombstones of this gloomy spot. They instead will let others perform that task so those folks can see for themselves if Lizzie Gould's ghost is real or not.

GHOSTS OF PENN'S WOODS

The haunted cemetery where Lizzie Gould is buried (2 views)

View of Lizzie's tombstone in the haunted cemetery.

GHOSTS OF PENN'S WOODS

The old church where Lizzie's ghost is sometimes seen.

R. B. WINTER STATE PARK

Located in Bald Eagle State Forest of Union County, this beautiful spot is noted for its Rapid Run Natural Area, but also not to be missed is its boiling spring. Little Bubbler, as this naturally-occurring artesian well is called, is notable for the way cold water seeps up from its underground aquifer and, ironically enough, causes the sand in the small pool of crystal clear liquid to appear to boil and "bubble". But the natural wonder goes largely unnoticed by park visitors, many of whom are probably not even aware that it exists. Likewise, the same might be said of the park's ghost, which seems to be a secretive one since it only made its presence known about five years ago.

Fifty-five years ago the park was known by a different title. Then known as Halfway Dam State Park, its name was based on several local landmarks. The first part of the name came from an old wayside inn called the Halfway House that stood here when the park grounds were purchased by the state in 1905. The inn itself had been given its designation from the fact that it sat midway along the 14-mile-long Brush Valley Narrows, a route traversed by PA Route 192 today and which connects the towns of Livonia, Centre County, and Forest Hill, Union County. But back in that time there was also an old sawmill dam on the spot, and it was that landmark from which the park got the second half of its title before the entire name was changed in 1957 to honor long-time District Forester Ray Winter who devoted a large part of his life to the upkeep and protection of this place.

GHOSTS OF PENN'S WOODS

Here today the waters of Rapid Run and Halfway Run fill a more modern dam, forming a six-acre lake which is used as a nice "swimmin' hole for locals in the summer months and fine trout fishing for anglers in fishing season. The 400 acres of park land, and many more acres of surrounding Bald Eagle State Forest land, also attract hikers who like to enjoy the cool heights of nearby Naked Mountain, Sand Mountain, and Seven Notch Ridge. But with so many "miles to wander", there are many potential hiding spots here as well; secluded sanctuaries that a ghost just might find inviting.

Among the dark hollows and other mystic places of the dense woodland that borders the stretch of Route 192 that runs through the park, there is none that looks more haunted than the park land along the last big turn just east of the dam. Here, where Brush Hollow Trail cuts through the deep woods, the rhododendron bushes grow profusely, and those, along with the many tall trees here, keep the forest floor in shadow, even at midday. It just may be an ideal spot for a ghost, and there are those who believe that one woman's ghostly encounter here seems to confirm this speculation.

The young lady had just completed her 3:00 PM to 11:00 PM shift at Lewisburg Evangelical Hospital one July night in 2005 and was heading back along Route 192 to her home in Rebersburg, Centre County. It had been one of those July "dog days", and the oppressive heat and humidity had turned into a downpour at 6:30 that afternoon. The deluge lasted until about 9:30 that night, but much of the earliest rain had turned to heavy fog when it met the hot asphalt paving of the highway. The mists were so thick that it was like a scene from a Hollywood horror movie as the tired hospital worker was forced to creep along Route 192 at a "snail's pace", even though she was the only car on the road at this late hour. But the slow speed, she realized, afforded her a chance to indulge in a more pleasant activity, and so she took the opportunity to roll down her car windows so she could enjoy the smell of the summer rain and the fresh scents of the rain-soaked forest. She had always liked the fragrances of campfires and any other odors that reminded her of the woods, and tonight was just another opportunity to enjoy some of them.

Although the dense fog caused her to drive more slowly than usual, the late-night traveler was also worried about deer crossing the road at this hour too, and when that thought came to mind she slowed down even more. By this time it had taken her about twenty minutes to reach Raymond B. Winter Park after passing through Forest Hill, and it was then that she reached a sharp turn in the road. She decelerated to navigate the curve, but after coming through it she was surprised to find that the road ahead was clear for some distance before the fog was blanketing it again. But she was even more surprised as her car came out of the curve and her headlight beams illuminated the right side of the highway.

At first she thought it was just a patch of white fog that had drifted out of the deep woods on the left or had rolled onto the road from off the steep mountain on the right, but when she looked again she realized that the "cloud" now appeared to be the figure of an eight or nine year old girl who was running at top speed in order to cross the highway. Caught completely off guard by the sight, the driver's initial reaction was to wonder what a little girl of that age was doing out by herself this late and on a bleak night like this. But then the bemused woman realized that although she could see some of the figure's distinguishing characteristics quite clearly, she could also see completely through it, almost like looking through a slightly translucent pane of glass.

Despite the fact that her glimpse into the unknown lasted less than a minute, it was distinct enough for the shaken onlooker to see that the colorless impression was that of a barefooted girl wearing an old-fashioned dress with puffy sleeves, and her hair styled in "pig tails". This "image of air", as it might be described, looked like someone from another century; a resident of an earlier time when women dressed in that way. But the young lady now appeared to be frightened. She never looked back at the perplexed woman who was staring at it in disbelief, but instead only seemed to be interested in getting away from its observer, or from unseen attackers, as quickly as possible. It was almost as though she were running for her life, and as far as the driver of the car was concerned, she wanted to get away as quickly as possible too. It had finally dawned on her that she had just seen a ghost, and she didn't want to tarry in this lonesome and inhospitable section of the mountains if it meant her only companion was to be someone from the spirit world.

GHOSTS OF PENN'S WOODS

There have been no other reported sightings of the ghost in recent years, nor are there any historical accounts or local legends that explain why it might be here in the first place. That's not a satisfying or happy ending to those who want to know more, but no ghost story ever satisfies the curious seeker who is looking for proof that life goes on in the next world. There never is a conclusive ending to such tales because all clues embedded in them are faint ones; it's as though we can only barely hear the footfalls from the threshold of that unknown place. And so it seems that the little Halfway Dam ghost will always be left to her wanderings. On the other hand, perhaps she will find peace one day, if she hasn't already. But if she is not yet at rest then maybe she will reappear from time to time to those who wish to solve her mystery and hope to penetrate the boundaries of the world that awaits us all.

GHOSTS OF PENN'S WOODS

The deep dark woods that is home to the ghost girl.

GHOSTS OF PENN'S WOODS

Sharp turn along Route 192 where the ghost girl appeared.

GHOSTS OF PENN'S WOODS

White mist and an orb? (right side of picture by the tree) in the haunted forest along Brush Hollow Trail and beside the sharp turn shown on the previous photo. This is the deep woods from which the apparently-frightened ghost girl came late one night in 2005.

WORLDS END STATE PARK

Visitors to Worlds End State Park may sometimes be drawn here solely on the basis of its title. The designation conveys an impression that this place is the proverbial "back of the Great Beyond" that adventurers sometimes refer to, but, although it is almost a wilderness in some places yet today, there is still some uncertainty about why it was named the way it was. There are some who say the name is a corruption of "Whirl's End", and that the area was originally referred to in that way because of a whirlpool that once was an unusual feature of the creek, Loyalsock Creek, which flows through here. Others say that the name "Worlds End" came from the opinions of the first travelers who journeyed into this wilderness and thought they had reached the end of the world since it was so inhospitable and impassable. Whatever the case may be, the Worlds End label won out after the whirlpool disappeared, and it does seem the more appropriate of the two options, given the landscape that is still here today.

Sullivan County is home to two state parks, with Ricketts Glen claiming some of its real estate and Worlds End lying totally within the rugged terrain known as Pennsylvania's Endless Mountains. That descriptive title is well placed, given the many mountain vistas that await the visitor to this part of the state, and Worlds End boasts a notable overlook of its own. The view requires a hike up the park's Canyon Vista Trail, but the effort will reward trekkers with a spectacular panorama of the Loyalsock Creek Gorge and other parts of the area known locally as the Sullivan Highlands. But the park and its surroundings have other noteworthy attractions as well, including a haunted lake to the south.

Within the park there is an assembly of monumental boulders that are another of the park's natural wonders. Access to The Rock Garden, as it's styled, is another plus for those who hike up the Canyon Vista Trail to the grand overlook. The gigantic rocks in the "garden" form a baffling and impressive maze that provide an interesting diversion for those who want to explore wild and mysterious places. But there is a similar spot just east of the park that will be appreciated by rock lovers as well.

The Haystacks, as they're called, can be found protruding from the waters of Loyalsock Creek along Route 220 just north of Laporte. The view of these rocky natural wonders requires navigating some moderately rugged trails to reach them, but once there the hiker can see that they do resemble small old-fashioned haystacks; the kind Little Boy Blue of nursery rhyme fame fell asleep under. A view of Dutchman's Falls at this same spot is yet another reward for making the trek back here, but if it's ghosts you're after then you need to return to Worlds End State Park and then head south to nearby Eagles Mere.

The story of the ghosts of Eagles Mere Lake, although not widely known today, has not been forgotten over the years because an account of their existence is preserved in the pages of an old diary that was kept by William Herndon, bookkeeper for George Lewis. Lewis was the owner of the glass works that once stood near the lake in the early 1800's, and at that time the body of water was known as Lewis' Lake, in honor of its owner. Normally a peaceful and relaxing place, the small lagoon, just as it does today, offered a cool retreat for those who wanted to enjoy some swimming and boating during the hot days of summer. However, its waters, if not respected, could be unforgiving to those who were foolish enough to disrespect them.

Dangerous seas were not on the minds of the young people who came to the lake that pleasant afternoon in August of 1809. In addition to Mrs. Lewis and her sister, young William Herndon was there with his wife of just two months. His Clara had come as a summer visitor to the Lewis household the previous year, and for him it had been love at first sight. Their "days of delight", as he would record it in his diary, throughout that summer of 1808 included pleasant explorations of "glens, caverns, and laurel bowers", and the young couple also enjoyed trips onto the lake to listen to "melodious warblings of the birds". The summer romance blossomed and in June of 1809 William and Clara were married. The match was everything the newlyweds had dreamed of, but in July of 1809 trouble had arrived in the form of Clara's younger brother, and now he was with them at the lake.

The reckless young man was not the type of person who was concerned about his own safety, and that was also true of anyone he happened to be with. He seemed to seek out and defy danger, and in one of his daredevil stunts he had managed to convert one of the lake's rowboats into a sailboat. That afternoon he had led his friends to the lake to see his creation, and now he was trying to convince them to take a sail with him. It took awhile but eventually his sister Clara, and Mrs. Lewis and her sister all succumbed to his charms and sailed out to the middle of the lake in the makeshift schooner. Then, seemingly out of nowhere, strong gusts of wind, precursors to a sudden and unexpected storm, capsized the craft.

Mrs. Lewis and her sister clung to the overturned boat, as did Clara's brother, but Clara had not been able to hold on, and her husband could not reach her before she disappeared into the dark green waters of the lake. He did manage to rescue the others, rowing each one ashore and then returning to get the next one, but he could not find his wife despite repeated attempts to do so. It was hard for him to accept the loss of his true love that day, and he would later record in his diary that he went back to the lake that night to mourn her, keeping a lonely vigil while sitting on the rocks overlooking the spot in the lake where she drowned.

Whether it was the feverish imaginings of a distraught husband or something else entirely, Herndon would note that in the moonlight at midnight that night, the mists, looking like a funeral shroud covering the surface of the lake, formed themselves into an image of Clara. The vision, he recorded, "Is that of Clara, gliding rather than walking over the water". At that point Herndon appears to have abandoned his diary, for there are no more of his personal entries in it after that fateful nocturnal reunion. However, his friend Charles Holmes did add some footnotes that will interest the ghost hunter.

Herndon's sighting of his wife's specter was a "tipping point" of sorts, or at least it may explain why, according to Holmes' notes, the bereaved husband "set his worldly affairs in order". Then, not too long afterwards, Herndon asked his friend to accompany him on another one of his nightly vigils. Strong gusts of wind buffeted the men as they sat on the rock, and at midnight Herndon claimed he could see his wife's image once more. Then, as Holmes strained his eyes to see the ghostly vision in the darkness, Herndon dove into the water, swam out to the spot where his wife had drowned, and, exhausted and waterlogged, sank into the murky depths of the choppy waters. There had been no time for Holmes to react, and several weeks later the bodies of both Herndon and his wife were recovered and buried in a nearby cemetery.

Intrigued by the unexpected and macabre events, Holmes and a friend returned to the rock one night several weeks later to see if Clara Herndon's spirit would appear to them. Their patience was finally rewarded when, at midnight, they could see, as he would footnote in Herndon's diary, "two misty forms upon the water coming toward us". To the onlookers the misty forms were not just exaggerated products of their imaginations. Holmes counteracted any such claims by also recording in the diary that "we clearly discerned Herndon and his wife gliding hand in hand, and that it is my belief that anyone who chooses to watch on the rock until midnight, in a true inquiring spirit, will see them appear again."

GHOSTS OF PENN'S WOODS

If not for the diary that was found in a hidden compartment of George Lewis' desk, the story of the ghosts of Eagles Mere Lake and its "Lover's Rock", as it's now referred to, may have been forgotten long ago. But now that, through this book, the story will become better known there will be those who want to investigate matters for themselves. The good news in that regard is that anyone who wishes to find the same rock and conduct their own vigil "in a true inquiring spirit" can do so today since the site can still be found along the shores of Eagles Mere Lake. It only takes a short hike down a well-worn trail along the eastern lakeshore, but it can be an unnerving hike for the faint of heart. The narrow Laurel Path, as locals call it, cuts through areas that are overgrown with almost impenetrable stands of Rhododendron, which add a mysterious and forbidding atmosphere to this lakeside glen. It is a feeling that becomes especially acute in those places where the bushes are so dense that they form an arch over the trail, thereby turning the pathway into nothing more than a dark tunnel. Needless to say, it would not be a very inviting place at midnight (see following photo of the Laurel Path and the orbs that appeared on it when the photo was taken during September of 2009).

GHOSTS OF PENN'S WOODS

Orbs along the Laurel Path that leads to Eagles Mere Lake

GHOSTS OF PENN'S WOODS

*Lover's Rock along the shore of Eagles Mere Lake
And view of the lake from atop Lover's Rock*

GETTYSBURG 1

Almost anyone who has visited Gettysburg National Military Park seems to go away with a sense that there is a different feeling to this place. Even though it is hallowed and consecrated ground, there is an air of melancholia here; a distinct sensation that these peaceful killing fields may be home to spirits that have not yet found their own peace. But that should not be surprising when it's considered that over 50,000 Federal and Confederate soldiers ended up as battlefield casualties during the three-day clash that started on the first of July, 1863.

The pitched battle turned into a hellish inferno of artillery and musket smoke, whining minnie balls, suicidal bayonet charges, and vicious man-to-man fighting with soldiers firing at each other at point-blank range, and then, after running out of ammunition, using the stocks of their empty muskets as clubs. Accompanying this frenzy of death were the terrible sounds of battle, including roaring cannons dispersing their deadly artillery fire, wailing artillery shells, and whizzing pieces of larger rocks blown into tiny pieces of shrapnel. Amid this horrible roar of combat arose the inevitable shrieks, curses, and shouts of the combatants, and the unnatural cries of wounded and dying men and horses.

The conflict at Gettysburg was marked by all these typical battle sounds as well as the strident yells of soldiers as they charged into the fray, including the Pennsylvania Reserves with their distinctive battle cry and the Confederates with the train-whistle-like "Woo! Woo! Woo!" of their blood-curdling Rebel Yell. But coupled with the human component of the battle noise were the more deafening sounds of the ever-present cannons. Gut-wrenching blasts of canister shot, Whitworth bolts, and any other missiles that could be used to tear a man apart, made the very earth shake and rumble. In fact some accounts state that the intensity of the cannon fire was so great that its rolling thunder was heard one-hundred and ten miles away in Philadelphia and as far west as Pittsburgh.

There are those who say that the rumbling noises heard so far away during those first three days of July in 1863 were nothing more than thunderstorms, but others say that if the atmospheric conditions were just right, then maybe the sounds of battle could have traveled unusual distances. But regardless of who is right, the non-believers will have difficulty explaining the sounds heard one night by a young man who was returning home after visiting his sweetheart in the town of Gettysburg some forty years after the guns of the battle had fallen silent.

Charles Rosensteel was taking a shortcut through the battlefield since it was getting late, that July night around the "turn" of the 20th century. It had been a pleasant evening; another happy "courting" session with the woman who was to become his wife. But now that it was almost midnight the love-struck beau tried to walk a little faster back to his parents' house. The historic scenes he was passing probably didn't even enter his thoughts as he made his way down Hancock Avenue; he was accustomed to them.

GHOSTS OF PENN'S WOODS

His parents' house sat in the shadows of Big Round Top, the peak which figured so prominently during the battle, and, growing up there, he had become so familiar with all the other well-known sites on the battlefield that he hardly gave any of them a second thought anymore. But that night, just as he was passing that spot known as the Angle, the place where Pickett's Charge ended on the third of July, 1863, his reveries were interrupted by sounds of a battle in progress.

There were shouts and curses of angry men, blasts of cannon fire, and a stentorian voice that stood out from all the others. It was a commanding voice, the call of a leader, and his words, "Give 'em the cold steel boys", were clear and distinct. But as curious as they might be, the sounds, along with the eerie surroundings, were enough to make the hairs stand up on the back of the young man's neck, and he made a point to get away from the area as fast as he could. But those same hairs may have stood up again when Rosensteel would later be reminded about how men of Major General George Pickett's Division attacked and died at this spot on the third of July, 1863.

During the famous charge that was to become the turning point of the whole Gettysburg engagement, the elite core of Robert E. Lee's Army of Northern Virginia, once described as "the flower of Virginia manhood", marched toward Union forces positioned a mile away behind stone walls on the hill known as Cemetery Ridge. For many of these brave southern soldiers it would be their last fight, as Federal cannons, which had maintained an eerie silence immediately before the Confederate onslaught began, now poured a merciless fire of shot and shell down upon the advancing lines of men. Canister and grapeshot cut huge gaps in the wavering lines of attackers, but the Rebels kept coming until they made it to a stone wall amid a clump of trees.

It was a location that was to become known as "The High Water Mark of the Confederacy"; a description used to indicate that this was the deepest penetration of Union lines achieved by Confederate troops during the battle. Out of 10,000 troops who began the assault, about 150 got to the stone barrier, only to be shot down or taken prisoner; and among the casualties was General Lewis Armistead, one of the bravest generals of the southern cause.

Soldiers on both sides would later recall seeing Armistead, his cap on his raised sword, stepping over the wall as he shouted, just before being mortally wounded, "Give 'em the cold steel boys! Who will follow me?" They are words that historians, to this day, still associate with this spot, and the sounds may be so indelibly imprinted on the fabric of space and time here that visitors just might still be able to hear them some hot night during the midnight hour on the third of July.

GHOSTS OF PENN'S WOODS

Monuments and cannons at the High Water Mark

Historical plaque at the High Water Mark showing sights and sounds of the battle at the stone wall on July 3, 1863

GETTYSBURG 2

Those who talk about the ghosts of Gettysburg are almost always referring to the spirits of the battlefield; vaporous images of Union and Confederate soldiers who were killed here during the terrible struggle of July 1 through 3, 1863, and who still haunt the places where they fell. However there are other phantoms that surface from time to time in the town environs, and these specters can be those of non-combatants; long-deceased innocent bystanders or townsfolk whose ethereal vestiges, for one reason or another, are still tied to the community and the battlefield. In fact in recent years it seems these same ghostly denizens have become almost as much of a tourist attraction as the battlefield itself. But tourists who come here are often at a loss when deciding where to start looking for the elusive phantoms, despite the many books that have been published on the subject. Nonetheless, there seems to be a consensus among Gettysburg's paranormal investigators that, out of all the ghost-inhabited places here, one of the most likely spots to see some of those spirits is in the Farnsworth House on Baltimore Street, downtown Gettysburg.

Built in 1810, the house served as a private residence for Harvey Sweeney's family at the time of the battle. Life in this small country town must have been idyllic in those days, at least up until that fateful July when Union and Confederate forces started a fight that neither side wanted nor had planned for. But once the battle began, the Sweeney's lives, as well as the lives of other townsfolk, would be affected in ways they had never thought possible. For the Sweeneys, the trouble began when Confederate troops took over their house.

The Rebels knew that this position afforded them a good prospect of nearby Cemetery Ridge, and they realized that as long as they held the house their snipers would have clear and unimpeded views of Union soldiers defending that elevation. The well-placed sharpshooters soon began to discharge their muskets from the loft and open upper back porch of the household, and their volleys proved to be deadly and disastrous for the Union troops on the hill that was to become such a key part of the battle. It was also one of those misdirected musket balls that mortally wounded young Jennie Wade, the only civilian killed during the battle. The bullet hole of that same ball can still be seen in the door of the nearby Jennie Wade House, which is also said to be haunted by the unfortunate young woman's ghost.

Union forces did not stand idly by and let the Confederate challenge go unanswered. They soon let loose a return fire that peppered the Sweeney's house and its unwanted guests with a hail of musket balls. Even throughout the night the sparkle of musket discharges lit up the town like so many fireflies, and by the next morning it seemed that the snipers were gone. Those making a closer inspection expected to find dead Rebel sharpshooters lying in the loft where they had been shot while drawing a bead on their attackers. However, there is uncertainty today as to whether any corpses were found there at all. Some think there were, others say not, but if not then it was a surprising result when it's considered that the outside wall of the room was riddled with over a hundred bullet holes, many of which can be seen there yet today.

After the battle a new owner renamed the Sweeney home the Farnsworth House in tribute to Union Army Brigadier General Elon John Farnsworth, who died leading a cavalry charge near Little Round Top on the third day of the battle. Today the Farnsworth House has been given the distinction of being the seventh most haunted inn in America. Its fourteen ghosts, some of which may be those of snipers who died in the loft above the Sara Black Room, are said to haunt the Inn's nine elegant Victorian guest rooms as well as the basement. The spirits have been there a long time, and so seem to like it here, but so do the many tourists who stay overnight just to meet these otherworldly guests.

It seems that most of those who stay in the Inn do not go away disappointed when it comes to experiencing paranormal activity. Accounts of their possessions being moved in the middle of the night; feelings that someone is touching them; sounds of disembodied voices and footsteps; mists and orbs appearing in photos, are all typical reports of those who have stayed here. Even ghost sightings surface now and again, but one of the most charming spirits of the place seems to be one that appeared to a pregnant young woman back in 2002.

The young nurse and her husband were staying in the Sara Black Room during that January night, while her parents and her husband's brother and his wife and children were lodged in other rooms in the house. They were all planning to go to a local restaurant for supper, but she was not feeling well. It was turning out to be a difficult pregnancy for her, and she told the others that she would stay behind while they went out. They had been reluctant to leave her alone, but she had been insistent and so they left. The uncomfortable mother-to-be immediately settled down in a reading chair in the room, turned on the reading lamp, and opened up a book she had started the day before.

Soon she was engrossed in her story, but she paused once in a while to rest her eyes or to take a sip from the bottle of Gatorade she had set down on the reading table beside her. Although the reading and her pregnancy may have relaxed her to the point of being drowsy, she was jolted back to full consciousness when she looked up one more time and saw her mother standing on the landing just outside the open door of the room. It surprised her to see her parent coming back alone, and she wondered why. When she asked her where the children were, the woman replied that they were outside running around the house. It seemed like an odd response, but the young nurse was also impressed by how strange her mother's white hair looked in the yellow glow of the reading lamp.

The perplexed young woman, still somewhat convinced that it was her mother she was looking at, continued to talk with her. Then, saying she needed to say goodbye, the visitor turned and walked away. It wasn't until the next morning that the young lady saw her mother again, but when she mentioned their previous night's conversation she was surprised when the matriarch denied that she had come back to the house alone and had not spoken to her at all. At first the puzzled daughter thought her mother was joking, but then as she began to think about the strange encounter she realized that the old-fashioned blue denim dress the woman she had spoken to was wearing was not the dress her mother had on when she went out.

That realization triggered yet another; a sudden inspiration that, although her nighttime visitor appeared to be flesh and blood, their conversation was more telepathic than verbal. It was then that the girl also realized that she must have seen one of the ghosts of the Farnsworth House. Still, it had not been a frightening experience. Thinking back she found it to be more of a comforting one, especially since it was accompanied by a faint smell of roses. The ghost, she now recalled, had even told her its name. She said she was called Mary when in human form, and she had also been a nurse; a caregiver for the children who once were kept in a nursery in the very same room.

Not long afterwards that day the young woman, upon seeing the familiar face of one of the innkeepers, asked her about the ghost she was sure had appeared before her the previous evening. The older lady was not surprised, recalling that others had seen Mary's ghost as well and that the apparition was always accompanied by the smell of roses. Furthermore, she noted, Mary seemed to be a helpful spirit with good intentions, especially toward pregnant women. It was for that reason, she explained, that, knowing the young nurse was having so many ill effects from being pregnant, she had prayed to Mary to take care of her and her baby. She had not anticipated how effective her prayers would be.

So there are those who are convinced even yet today that the comforting spirit of the former nurse known as Mary is compelled to remain in the Farnsworth House. The reason, they say, may be that she is disquieted by the spirits of Confederate sharpshooters that are said to still haunt the loft above her room. Their presence perhaps makes her feel that she needs to protect any babies or children that sleep there; have caused her motherly instincts to become so strong that they have overwhelmed her sensibilities and make her think she is still alive and needed. On the other hand, maybe she can never rest as long as the bullet holes, still there on the outside wall of the Inn, remain as reminders of the terrible things that happened in the house during the Battle of Gettysburg.

GHOSTS OF PENN'S WOODS

The Farnsworth House

GHOSTS OF PENN'S WOODS

The bullet holes (white marks) on the side of the Farnsworth House and the snipers' window in the attic.

Landing and door into the Sara Black Room in the Farnsworth House (the unusual carving of the boar's head on the wall lends an even more other-worldly feeling to this spot where Mary's ghost was seen by the young nurse)

GHOSTS OF PENN'S WOODS

Ghostly orb in the Farnsworth House attic

While my wife and I were touring the attic in October of 2010, my wife's hair was caressed by unseen fingers, my camera mal-functioned, and this orb appeared over my head on a photo taken of me by another member of our party! Perhaps the orb is a camera artifact caused by the light bulb or maybe it's confirmation that snipers died here after all! It was a totally unexpected yet thrilling climax to our weekend, and one that will draw us back here again! (Photo courtesy of Vikki Barker)

SCOTIA BARRENS

Also identified as State Game Lands 176, this historic tract of forestland in the rapidly-growing area surrounding State College in Centre County has long been considered unique. The Indians who were the first inhabitants here considered it so after they tried to cultivate its soil and found it to be unfit for agricultural pursuits. White settlers soon learned the same hard facts, and they too left "The Barrens", as it came to be known, in the hands of the Tanglewood Gods. Left on its own, the region was soon overgrown with pitch pine, scrub oak, hemlocks, and thick stands of Rhododendron bushes; vegetation so thick that, no matter how sunny the day even today, dark shadows always seem to be trying to conceal the many ponds and wetlands that are scattered through here. On the other hand, there are those who say those same shadows may be hiding something else: the black ghost that is said to make the Barrens its home. But much to the delight of locals, the presence of a ghost does not ruin the area's many other attractions.

Now classified as a Biological Diversity Area, the Barrens is home to rare specifies of both flora and fauna, offering many opportunities for hikers, bird watchers, joggers, and others who just want to enjoy a peaceful interlude in the woods. And those who will wait and watch may catch a glimpse of whitetail deer, wild turkeys, ruffed grouse, or even a black bear or two. But it wasn't always that way.

Decades after the Indians moved away, white settlers began to resettle this section, finding natural resources here that were ideal for their own industries. Consequently, The Barrens became even more desolate-looking as the years went by. Tar pits and charcoal operations seemed to sprout up faster than plants of the edible kind. The area's majestic virgin pine trees, which once thrived on the acid soil, were cut down and used to supply the many charcoal furnaces that were erected here and whose cheery fires glowed continuously, day and night. Despite the advances of the Industrial Revolution, advancements in agricultural science did not reveal any secrets for profitably farming on soils like those found in The Barrens, and so the area seemed to be resolutely determined to yield little or nothing of value to those who dared to coax more than a meager living from it.

That was soon to change, particularly after the end of the Revolutionary War when large deposits of iron ore were discovered in The Barrens, and mining operations began in earnest. The desolate territory that had once proved so inhospitable, and that had appeared reluctant to support human endeavors of any kind, seemed at last to begrudgingly pour forth its riches upon those who would dig for them, including Pittsburgh steel magnate Andrew Carnegie.

Carnegie's steel company began buying up land in the area in 1880, and soon erected an ore processing plant, along with company houses that would become the nucleus of the town that he renamed Scotia, after his native Scotland. Soon two neighboring towns, River Hill and Marysville, came into existence as more iron workers moved into the area. During this period of economic good times, the number of people living in and around Scotia peaked at 450 to 500, but Scotia's brief day in the sun eventually faded into dusk as the ore plant became too expensive to operate.

Thirty years after they came into existence, the villages of Scotia, River Hill, and Marysville became ghost towns when iron operations closed for good, victim of larger quantities of higher quality ore found along the Great Lakes in Minnesota. The harsh economic realities of the times forced people to leave The Barrens for employment elsewhere, and so the area was left once again to grow up in scrub oak, pitch pine, and similarly-unattractive undergrowth such as hawthorn bushes, poison sumac, and deadly nightshade.

Memories of the old iron ghost towns lasted as long as their former residents, but eventually even these recollections faded away as the original inhabitants died off. Junk dealers gradually carted away the machinery that once processed vast quantities of rich iron ore, and wood from some of the houses that were the now-deserted homes of Carnegie employees was used to build barns in the surrounding countryside. In fact, it wasn't too long until only foundations remained to mark the site of this once-thriving boomtown. The Barrens was once again a lifeless place, left to the mercy of its old Nemesis - the forest fires that often swept through the trees, leaving the ground as black as the sable coat of night.

But those same fires did more than temporarily blacken the landscape of The Scotia Barrens. The soot of those infernos darkened a soul as well; one that was already blackened before the forest fires returned to The Barrens. For there is a restless ghost that haunts the hills around the old iron ghost towns - a soul that can find no rest due to the dastardly deeds it committed when it was flesh and blood, and which, when it appears to others, manifests itself not as a typical pale spirit, but one whose vapors are the color of soot.

Black clouds did seem to be gathering over the crest of nearby Gatesburg Ridge during the start of Scotia's economic slide in 1910. Even the outlines of the Bald Eagle Mountains to the north appeared darker and more foreboding as the harsh realities of the times became apparent and started to weigh on men's minds. Then in October of that same year a sensational murder took place in The Barrens - a murder that would lead to the arrest, conviction, and hanging of a black man named Bert Delige.

Delige was no choir boy. He had spent time in prison twice before - once for voluntary manslaughter in western Pennsylvania, and another time for attempted armed robbery at John Haugh's grocery store in Scotia. During this last escapade, Delige had shot at Haugh but had wounded the storekeeper's nephew instead. Now the easily-inflamed ex-con was about to commit his last crime in the bone-chilling air of an October night in 1910.

To this day The Barrens is noted for fall and winter temperatures that can be up to thirty or forty degrees lower than the country around it - a phenomena that's caused by the gradual absorption of cold air by the iron deposits in the ground, which then act like a giant ice cube. But even though the weather was cold, that night in 1910, the sky was exceptionally clear and the light of a full moon bathed farmlands and woodlands in an eerie yellow glow that made it seem like it was still daytime. It was so well lit that Mrs. Hulda Baudis, 51-year-old widow of John Baudis, decided it was safe enough to take a short cut past the old mud dam when she started to walk back home after a visit with her sister. But fate had other plans that night.

The black man lying in wait in a cornfield near her house had once worked for her husband, the well-known "merry-go-round man" of Centre County, and he had long claimed that the Baudis's still owed him back wages. But John Baudis, and now his widow, had refused to consider Bert Delige's claims, and Delige had drunk himself into a towering rage that Sunday evening. His rage grew as he waited for his victim, and when she was finally near enough he jumped out of his hiding place among the corn rows. After overpowering and raping her he let her up and started to flee, but she called out his name as he ran away, saying she would see that he would pay for what he had done. It was that threat that pushed Delige over the edge. Turning around he grabbed the helpless woman and calmly slit her throat with a straight razor he was carrying in his pocket.

It took nearly six months before Bert Delige paid for his crime, but pay he did after overwhelming evidence led to his conviction and a sentence of death by hanging. The execution on April 25, 1911, went off without incident, and his body was taken back to The Barrens and interred in non-hallowed ground.

Instead of being buried in the nearby Negro cemetery - segregation was even a practice that applied to the dead in those days - Delige's corpse was placed in a grave near the Delige homestead. No service was conducted, and a simple, unmarked, flat stone was placed over the internment site. That seemed to settle the matter once and for all; justice had been served. However, even though the public mind was satisfied, it would seem that Bert had other ideas.

Sixty-one years after Bert Delige was hanged in the Bellefonte jail yard, a carload of teenagers decided to have some fun on a cold October night in 1972, and they chose a remote spot in the Scotia Barrens to have their party; next to one of Andrew Carnegie's abandoned ore pits, which was now filled with water. One of the boys had stolen some cigarettes and beer from his father, and now he and his girlfriend, along with another couple, were "making out"; one couple inside the car and one outside in the front. A third teenager, who was acting as the chauffeur (we'd call him a "designated driver" today) for the two couples, had gotten out of the vehicle and wandered off into the nearby woods.

Then, just as things were heating up, the young man on the ground in front of the car jumped up on the hood while calling for his chauffeur friend. He seemed terrified and kept yelling about "a big black beast" in the woods on the other side of the ore pit. The cries startled the young man in the back seat of the car, and it took him several seconds before his eyes focused on the mysterious intruder. But what he saw and what happened next would stay with him for the rest of his life.

The third young man had quickly gotten into the driver's seat, and he now wasted no time in backing the car away from the pit. The car's tires sent stones and dirt flying as the driver screamed that a black mist was forming in front of the car. He somehow managed to turn the vehicle around, and as it sped away the young man in the backseat looked behind them. There, standing on the ridge by the large water-filled pit, was a black silhouette of a man, who appeared to be holding a large knife.

There are those who say that the teens were scared off that October night by one of the black bears that call the Barrens home, but the young man who saw the black silhouette still claims that it was a human shape and not that of an animal. Certainly the month of the sighting is also suggestive, given that it is the month that Delige committed his crime, and so today's ghost hunter may find this area to be a fertile one when looking for evidence of life beyond the grave. However, it would appear that the best time to come would be on a cold October night when the sky is crystal clear and a full moon casts a ghostly light on the dark and lonesome shadows that seem to be a prominent feature of this deserted place.

Site of the old mud dam
Scotia Barrens, Centre County

GHOSTS OF PENN'S WOODS

Bert Delige's resting place
Scotia Barrens, Centre County

GHOSTS OF PENN'S WOODS

Place where the black ghost was seen
Scotia Barrens, Centre County

PINE CREEK GORGE

Better known as Pennsylvania's "Grand Canyon", the scenic Pine Creek Gorge in north-central Pennsylvania has been designated as a National Natural Landmark by the National Park Service. Sitting within 160,000 acres of Pennsylvania's Tioga State Forest, the impressive chasm starts in Wellsboro, Tioga County, and ends fifty miles to the south near Waterville in Lycoming County. The area's protected status has kept it in an undeveloped and natural state since preservation efforts began in the 1920's, and today two State Parks located on both the west and east sides, or "rims", of the canyon, offer hikers many "miles to wander", either along the rim trails or down in the gorge itself.

Geologists say the declivity was formed over 350 million years ago through the combined action of glaciers and unrelenting erosion by Pine Creek, which still flows along the bottom of the canyon today, providing sporting opportunities for fishermen, whitewater rafters, and canoeists. But hikers are also drawn here, attracted by the breathtaking views from the rim trails or by the views from the canyon floor, where canyon walls rise to a height of 1400 feet at the deepest point. And the views are available to anyone; can be enjoyed free of charge by current-day visitors to Colton Point State Park on the canyon's west rim or Leonard Harrison State Park on the east rim. But the unusual topography here was also a source of amazement to the local Indians. It was such an unusual place to them that they could only imagine that it must have been a special creation of their Great Spirit, who, they believed, must have dug it out with his tomahawk.

Those looking for spirits in the canyon today might think that a good place to start would be along the road leading into the western side of Colton Point State Park called Deadman Hollow Road. The name is certainly evocative of the spirit world, and would seem to support a belief that the gloomy depths of this uninviting spot may be home to a ghost; a restless and unsettled spirit that, for whatever the reason, cannot move on to its eternal home. And in fact the history behind the title of the roadway does support this idea as well, because it tells of a man named O'Conner who died a horrible death here sometime in the early 1900's.

His brothers were loggers in the area, and the O'Conner branch of nearby Fourmile Run, which flows through the park today, was named after them. But he made his living, or supplemented his income, in a more free-spirited way. He was a trapper, and along with foxes, beaver, and mink, he also trapped bear, and it was this last animal that led to his downfall. One day as he was setting his traps the experienced trapper let his guard down; did not pay attention to where he was walking. He may have realized it just before it happened, but there was no time to react as he stepped on the bear trap and its massive steel jaws clamped down on his leg.

He must have struggled and screamed for hours, but eventually thirst and exhaustion wore him down, and, unable to escape from his tether and out of hope that any rescuers would find him, he ultimately died of starvation and exposure. He must have lain there for weeks or months because his body was in an advanced state of decomposition when it was later found by some passing hunters. The event left an indelible impression upon the locals, who decided to name the hollow where the body was found after the gruesome discovery that was made there. It bears that name today, and there are those who say the area is haunted by O'Conner's spirit, perhaps because of its horrible death or because it feels the hollow should have been named O'Conner Hollow to better commemorate its memory.

But legends say there is also another restless spirit near here that met an even more horrible death when in human form, and which was even more frightening to local Indians when they heard its cries; cries that some believe can still be heard echoing off the Canyon's walls when the night winds begin to blow through the Gorge and moonlit shadows dance on the canyon floor and along the banks of Pine Creek.

Indians once frequented this area, using it as one of their prime hunting grounds for thousands of years. History states that they even had a path that ran the entire length of the great gorge; a wilderness trail the early settlers here named the Pine Creek Path. But although the hardiest and bravest settlers traveled through the canyon they contended that the Indians avoided parts of it altogether; and they did so because they were afraid. The area is rich in Indian legend and lore, and one of their accounts seems to confirm the settlers' contentions; provides an explanation as to why the Indians may have had good reason to be afraid.

The Indians passed their story on to older residents of the area, who in turn preserved it for future generations, and according to that tale the place the Indians avoided was along the west rim of the canyon where the Bradley Wales Lookout is today. The old narrative begins back in the early 1600's when there was a period of drought that lasted three years, resulting in conditions so dry that the forest was nothing more than a tinder box and massive forest fires became the norm. It was a time the Indians here would later call the time of the "Big Burn", and early 1800 lumber company records that preserved the ages of the trees they harvested here seem to support the fact that few trees older than 150 years old were found at that time, most of the others of that vintage presumably having been burnt up by the fires of the "Big Burn".

The Indians here at the time of the "Big Burn" experienced another problem in that the big fires wiped out all the wildlife here that they depended upon for food. It was a desperate situation and, in the minds of the Indians, it called for extreme measures. According to the old tale the measure they decided upon was to take the child of one of their unwed mothers and sacrifice it to the rain god. Their reasoning was that this would surely induce their rain god to send down the rainfall they so desperately needed, and so one summer evening as the sun was sinking low in the western sky they took the chosen child to a place on the west rim of the canyon near present-day Bradley Wales Lookout and threw it over the side.

The old account says that the poor babe's screams could be heard until it had fallen all the way to the bottom of the canyon.

From that time on the Indians began to hear sounds like that of a baby crying when they passed by here at sunset in the summertime. Eventually the sounds became so unnerving that the sons of the forest avoided the spot altogether. It was too frightening for them; too harsh a reminder of the awful event that occurred here and the wrathful spirit that may have been the result.

There are those who have heard the crying sounds at Bradley Wales in recent times, and they say it's most audible on summer evenings at the south end of the overlook where an old wagon road once came down off of it. It's at that time and place, just as the wind and warm air in the canyon start to sweep through the canyon, that the sounds begin and increase in volume as the winds rise. It was a sound that scared the less-sophisticated Indians of four-hundred years ago; frightened them so badly that, just like their legend states, they more than likely did avoid this part of the canyon – this place they thought was haunted by the ghost of the wailing child.

However, the sounds still have the same impact on those who hear them today. Even though people now are more likely to attribute the "cries" to the sound of the wind going up through the rocks on the sides of Bradley Wales as colder air comes off the top of the mountain and sucks the warm air up over the canyon, those who have heard them are sometimes not so sure. The strange reverberations so closely resemble a baby's cries in fact that one person who has experienced them first hand had to admit that the first time he heard them "it made the hairs stand up" on the back of his neck. Those looking for a "ghostly" experience may want to decide for themselves whether the canyon cries are just sounds of the night wind or whether there's more to them than that.

View of the cliff of the wailing child from Bradley Wales Lookout along the west rim of the canyon

POE VALLEY 1

When twilight shadows begin to fade and stars start to twinkle in the sky above, Poe Valley State Park is a place where the lonesome call of the whippoorwill can still be heard in the darkening woods, and where, in the early summertime, the fireflies often light up the night with their strange luminescence. Here as well, especially on nights when blustery winds gust through the trees and toss silvery black clouds around in a moonlit sky, there can sometimes be heard the intimidating cries of coyote packs calling from the tops of nearby mountain peaks. The sounds are faint echoes of the past and reminders that all is not always as it may seem to be in this shadowy place; a place that creates an impression that it could be the abode of both the living and the dead. But the park is there for the living, and it has recently undergone an extensive renovation and remodeling project resulting in much-improved lakeside changing rooms for swimmers and new cabins for overnight rentals so that those who wish to experience a night in the woods without having to stay in a tent or camper can now do so.

However since the park has been modernized so much, those looking for ghosts here may feel that it's useless to expect to find any; think that any remnants of the spirit world have been dislodged and forced to find peace at some other remote spot in the mountain fastness that extend for miles and in all directions over this portion of Penn's Woods. While it is true that the park does not seem to have ever been able to claim a ghost of its own, there are nonetheless still opportunities for finding them nearby.

Along the forest roads leading into the park there are spots that have both historical and supernatural associations. Along Pine Swamp Road, for example, was once the infamous Pine Swamp and its white sand spring where the last wolf in the area was said to have been caught in a trap set by one of the early settlers here. Then, too, along Poe Paddy Drive (no longer maintained and advisable only for four-wheel drive vehicles or foot traffic), there are several spectacular views worth expending the effort to see. Among them is the impressive Penns View, which provides a panoramic overlook of Penns Valley and the small village of Ingleby nestled among the ridges below. It has a ghostly tale associated with it, as does the next overlook on the same road. Known to locals as Ravens' Knob, this second picturesque view has its own unique history and associated ghost story as well. Both tales add a touch of local color and human interest to the park, and both also will be of interest to those who are seeking ghosts here.

The account of the Ingleby "monster" began decades ago with the fishermen who, in the springtime during fishing season, could often be found dangling their lines in the cold waters of Penns, Elk, or Pine Creeks near the old railroad tunnel. That same tunnel can still be seen today at Tunnel Mountain, but those who live in the nearby villages of Coburn and Ingleby seem to avoid the place. Perhaps the reason is because it has a reputation for being home to the occasional rattlesnake, but maybe the reason goes back to those earlier fisherman, who, it was said, sometimes avoided the place as well. Somewhat closed-mouthed about the basis for the admonition, the anglers would often tell their younger counterparts that loafed with them at Coburn's country store that "You never go fishing down by the old railroad tunnel after dark".

Once hailed as "Centre County's foremost resort town", the tiny settlement of Ingleby was also once known for its bees, which, some say, were actually the basis for its name. It seems that an early settler named Ingle kept beehives here as a livelihood, and there are those that believe Ingle and his bees were the inspiration for the naming of the village. But over the years Ingleby has also achieved some notoriety for its monster, and the foundation of the old barn and farmhouse where the story began can still be seen in a lonesome clearing located on the hills that surround the little Penn Township town.

To those who saw it fifty years ago there was a decidedly weathered and wearied look about the place, as though its abandonment was not a recent one, and in fact that was the case. At least that's what was claimed in the local story that told of the horrible events that once supposedly occurred here sometime during the last decade of the nineteenth century or first decade of the twentieth.

Back then, in the days when the railroad came through the town and there was a hotel to accommodate vacationers who came to be reinvigorated by the fresh country air, it was a routine custom for many locals to go into the larger neighboring communities on Saturday nights to do their shopping and socializing. Saturday nights, therefore, meant the folks of Ingleby, and those who lived in the surrounding hollows, could often be found in the nearby villages of Coburn or Millheim enjoying their one and only "night on the town" for the week. And among the regulars was the family who lived in the house that seemed so far back in the woods, even in that sparsely settled age.

Neighbors here in those days were scarce, and so everyone looked out for one another in a general spirit of cooperation and mutual support. Therefore if a family failed to come to town on a Saturday night their absence was noted by someone; and so it was that on one Saturday night the absence of the hill hawks who lived out on the mountain was duly noted and often mentioned in passing conversations. However, when the family failed to show up again on the following Saturday night it was decidedly not a good sign, and so locals agreed that they should investigate.

When they got to the secluded homestead there was no one there, even though the table was set for the evening meal with dishes of hot food on the table. It seemed as though the family had been frightened away by something before they could sit down to the dinner; they had apparently fled in such haste, in fact, that they hadn't left a clue as to where they were going. It was a mystery that was never solved, and for several years the homestead remained unoccupied.

But then one day a stranger took up residence there. He was not a local and he seemed to like his privacy, but his neighbors tried to befriend him anyway, stopping by once in a while to say hello. But one day when someone went in to speak to him they found him beheaded. That, too, remained an unsolved mystery, at least according to the tale, but for the country folks of the area it was the proverbial "last straw".

It wasn't long before rumors started flying through the valley stating that there had to be some sort of demonic force or monster, cloaked in invisibility, menacing the town of Ingleby. The accounts also claimed to know where the monster made its home, and there, some believe, it still sleeps today, arising only when someone dares to trespass upon territory it has claimed for its own.

The haunted spot is thought to be in a copse of trees that stands on the side of a field along the old Millheim-Siglerville Pike. While scenic, the drive over the dirt mountain road on Big Poe Mountain is not for those who feel they need to be near human contacts. It is a remote and little-visited thoroughfare, and it has been that way since it was built. Today there are camps and even some houses along the stretches closest to the valleys the road connects, but back in earlier times there were few habitations along here. Nonetheless, a few of them can still be seen today, including an old country schoolhouse that was once a seat of learning for the local mountain children of Poe and Penns Valleys. Today the old school is a hunting camp, and it is in back of it that the field with its haunted copse of trees can be found, and, like the road itself, it is not an inviting spot at nighttime or even at sunset.

GHOSTS OF PENN'S WOODS

That fact was experienced first-hand by one teenager during hunting season back in the early 1960's. He had gone hunting in the mountains above Ingleby and Coburn in early October, during small game season, and it was just starting to get dark when he came out of the dark recesses of Stillhouse Hollow about a half mile from the old country schoolhouse (now Clover Hunting Camp). The solitary hunter was not uncomfortable about being alone in the woods, particularly while carrying a rifle, and so he was not unnerved when he thought he sensed, more than heard, something on the dirt road behind him. He turned and looked, but there was nothing there, and so he started out again. For awhile it seemed as though it had been his imagination, but when the sensation returned, only more strongly this time, he became concerned.

He had the distinct and unpleasant impression that whatever or whoever was behind him was closing in fast, and so he stopped and turned around a second time, determined to keep looking until he spotted his silent stalker. However once again he saw no trace of a mysterious follower, but then suddenly he experienced a cold chill spreading over his entire body and an unpleasant "clammy" sensation that almost felt like someone was trying to grab him. The feeling was overpowering, and thoughts of small game were forgotten as the frightened hunter sprinted out of the area. He has returned here in recent years, but for many years following his hair-raising experience he avoided this place of mystery; an area that local folktales say still may be haunted by the Ingleby Monster.

GHOSTS OF PENN'S WOODS

The scenic outlook at Penns View with the ghost town of Ingleby in the foreground and the railroad bridge spanning Penns Creek on the right.

GHOSTS OF PENN'S WOODS

The haunted woods and field which locals say are the playground of the Ingleby Monster.

POE VALLEY 2

As noted in the last chapter, there is a scenic overlook, known locally as Ravens' Knob, which can be found along one of the forest roads leading into Poe Valley State Park. This breathtaking view along Poe Paddy Drive has an interesting tale associated with it, but one made more intriguing because of the ghosts related to it. However, its roots are grounded in a much earlier time since it begins during an era when there were no automobiles or other similar modern-day conveniences which we take for granted today. In fact, to discover the reason for the view's name, and to reveal the ghosts associated with it, we must go back to the early 1800's when the stagecoach stopped in the nearby village of Potters Mills.

The large brick building that served as the stagecoach stop is still there today, but it's now sadly abandoned and deteriorating after serving for years as a restaurant. It's sad to see it in that condition, especially since it has a colorful history and a reputation as one of the most haunted inns in Pennsylvania. There are probably many interesting accounts about passengers who "laid over" at the brick hotel when it was a regular stop along the stage line that ran between Lewistown, Mifflin County, and Bellefonte, Centre County, but there is one in particular that still causes people to pause, and wonder.

This remarkable account claims that sometime in 1839 a Philadelphian got off the stage from Lewistown and requested a room at the hotel in the little town known at that time as Potters

Bank. Though not nearly as eminent in 1839 as he would become after he died ten years later, the irascible gentleman did have a number of published poems and stories to his credit; literary efforts that were characteristic of the many similar creations for which he was to become famous. Although the old inn at Potters Bank would have been a quiet setting for literary pursuits, the man's business was of a decidedly more practical nature, and these interests required him to journey back into the wildest parts of the somber mountains that seemingly stretched endlessly into the eastern horizon.

It was on a trip into these same mountains one day, proclaims the legend, that the young adventurer unexpectedly met a pretty mountain maid on a lofty and windy peak. It was "love at first sight" for the city boy, who was easily-enamored when first meeting any lovely young women, especially when the meetings occurred in lonely and out-of-the-way places like this. However, the local young beauty was not as easily smitten, and so the rejected suitor sought solace by wandering even deeper into the hills on a daily basis.

During one of his solitary trips into the woods the jilted paramour came to a panoramic overlook of range upon range of mountains, extending almost as far as the eye could see. At the base of the steep and rocky ledges of the overlook were miles and miles of dense forest which concealed deep dark hollows and a hidden valley that locals had name High Valley. What intrigued the depressed youth the most, however, or so the legend states, was the large number of birds that seemed to call the cliffs their home.

The fluttering avians looked like crows since they were as black and shiny as coal, but they were much larger cousins of those birds, and they did seem to like it here. The place was apparently their nesting ground, for the spot, the lone observer was later to find, had been named "Raven's Knob" after them. In fact, it was the mournful cries of the ravens and, on cloudier days, the weird charm of the spot that supposedly drew the disenchanted Philadelphian back to it time and time again.

It would have indeed been a place that was lonely and bleak enough to fit his own temperament at the time, and it would have no doubt inspired him, if the story is true. For it was here, claim the local tellers of the tale, that the despondent young poet was inspired to write one of his most famous compositions. At this spot, they claim, Edgar Allen Poe penned in entirety his poem entitled "The Raven". The tale is a disputed one since there are other areas of the state that also claim that their scenery was the inspiration for Poe's famous poem (see Trough Creek State Park), but the old stagecoach stop in Potters Mills (last known as the Eutaw House Restaurant) had a piece of furniture and at least one ghost that former owners sited as proof of the legitimacy of their claims to Poe's poem.

Perhaps the table is as old as the one-hundred and seventy-five year old building in which it stood, and if that is true, then its condition is not all that surprising. Blackened here and there with an occasional circular spot where, it is claimed by the hotel's past owners, patrons once ignited puddles of whisky in order to test the alcohol content of their drinks, the surface of the old relic is also covered with initials carved into it by bored travelers waiting for the next stage.

Curious onlookers who inspected the table and its numerous defacements would eventually notice a set of letters on one corner of the tabletop that were carved in characters bolder than the other inscriptions. At first the initials would have seemed to be the elusive proof that confirmed the legend of Poe's visit here, but while the letters, which appeared as *EAP*, are intriguing, they were not conclusive enough to say they were Poe's. Someone else with identical initials, or someone who was a fancier of the poet and the legend, could have whittled those same letters into the table top. But among the former employees of the place there is no doubt as to whether or not ghosts have visited the old stagecoach stop. They even say that some of those spirits have never left.

The Eutaw House has been an eventful paranormal spot for its employees. They even have a name for one of its most playful spirits. They call it Edgar's ghost, after the famous poet who supposedly stayed here in 1838, but he is just one of many other poltergeists who have plagued staff members over the years. Those willing to share their strange experiences say that poltergeist activities include pretzel jars and beer bottles sliding down the bar counter on their own. There have also been incidents where fifty pound crocks of salt and flour seemingly flew through the air as if thrown by unseen hands, and after one such event it took three staff members an hour to clean up the mess. Another time, when a pitcher flew out of the empty kitchen and landed at the bartender's feet, it was almost enough to cause her to hand in her resignation and leave. The poltergeists also like to make their presence known by scattering coasters, straws, toothpicks, chairs, and table settings after staff members closing for the night have arranged them for the next day's customers.

Former employees also recall the many cold spots that they've encountered when walking from room to room to do their jobs. These spine chilling spots are, they feel, evidence of the ghosts that reside here, including that of a lady in a long white antique-style dress who seems to make her home on the second floor. The image of the woman as she ascends the stairs has appeared to some as a reflection in an antique mirror hanging on the wall at the bottom of the stairs leading to the second floor. But one mother and daughter had a more personal encounter with her one day when they had come from Lewistown to enjoy a relaxing and delicious lunch.

After being seated, the young mother gave her daughter some sheets of white paper on which she could draw pictures while waiting for their food. In time, however, the little girl decided to visit the ladies room on the second floor, and when she returned her mother did the same. However, when the mother came back down she immediately asked the waitress about the employee she met in the ladies room who was wearing a long white antique-style dress. She said she had asked her if she worked here, and that she simply smiled, replied "No", turned away, and refused to answer any more questions. It had been a frightening experience for the young woman, especially after the waitress said no such person was employed there; but something even more unnerving was about to occur on her way home.

On the way back the little girl continued to draw, but then unexpectedly handed her mother the picture she had just finished, stating "Here's the lady I saw in the bathroom. She wouldn't talk to me!" The drawing was of an older woman in a long white antique-style dress.

There are no accounts that identify who the old lady's ghost might be, but there are accounts of other individuals who were supposedly murdered here, and so there's no telling which ones may turn up next or which ones make their presence known as poltergeists. Today they may wish only that the old place will open again soon so that they can once again prove to others that they are there and wish to stay.

One of the most haunted rooms in the Eutaw House where overnight guests in adjacent rooms have heard the water turn on and off at the sink, the toilet flush, and disembodied voices coming from within.

HAIRY JOHN'S

Near the eastern edge of Centre County, where its boundary line with Union County is defined, there is a natural gap, or "cut" through the mountains that connects the villages of Woodward, Centre County, and Hartleton in Union County. This gloomy defile, popularly known as the Woodward Narrows, is always filled with somber shadows in some of its deeper glens and hollows, and even at midday on some days the forest here is home only to whispering pines, restless oaks, and the soft murmur of Voneida Run as it courses through the cool mists of the dark forest. But according to local legends there is also a ghost that makes its home here; one that occasionally appears to unsuspecting nighttime motorists.

The area's lack of human habitation and the small amount of vehicular traffic through it can sometimes lend an otherworldly air and uninviting quality to the place, and it is at such times that few people choose to tarry here. But this quaint little corner of woodland is surrounded by acres of Bald Eagle State Forest, and so it holds many attractions for the nature lover. Hunters, hikers, campers, and picnickers all enjoy this mini-wilderness formed by the towering heights of Winkellblech, Sand, and Thick Mountains, and many folks take advantage of its refreshing forest breezes, nature's air conditioning, during the hottest days of summer. However there is one other attraction along the road here that many people find intriguing, and that's the signboard that advertises the roadside rest called Hairy John's State Forest Picnic Area.

GHOSTS OF PENN'S WOODS

Once a full-fledged state park, this peaceful forest glen was demoted due to lack of funding. Now the little-visited place has become a wayside curiosity, and the origins of its name are not that widely known anymore. But it's not really been that long ago that John Voneida could be found in his little cabin in the spot along the narrows that would later bear his name. Likewise, not too many decades ago there were people alive who, in the late 1800's, could still recall seeing the old hermit of the narrows come into the nearby village of Woodward to buy molasses, flour, and other staples in the shadow of the *Rundkupf*, or Roundtop Mountain.

It was a time when butchering, apple butter boiling, corn husking, and quaint mountain characters like Hairy John were part of everyday rural life here, but it's said that his quiet entrances into the sleepy little town were always a signal for the children there to run and hide from the hairy little man. Voneida's long hair and lengthy beard must have been intimidating to the youngsters, but it was probably the tales they had heard their parents tell about him that really made them afraid. For John Voneida's past was clouded by a dark secret; a terrible story that caused some to fear him.

Nasty rumors seemed to travel with the kindly recluse. There were insinuations that he had left his wife because of constant disagreements and other marital problems; abandoning her to live a solitary existence in the mountains. There were even harsher rumors that claimed that "he mistreated his wife or even killed her, but the diminutive recluse stoutly denied any such gossip.

GHOSTS OF PENN'S WOODS

The old legends don't say much more about his wife, other than there was a belief that she was mentally unstable or "feeble-minded as they labeled such people in those days. Those same old accounts claim that her mental state deteriorated to the point where her inner demons drove her to suicide, and that one day she hanged herself in a closet of the Voneida's homestead. But there were those townsfolk who said she had not committed suicide at all; that her husband had hung her himself.

Eventually the gossip and taunts were too much to bear, and he was eventually driven away from his native Nittany Valley to nearby Penns Valley, preferring a solitary life in the mountains to neighbors of any kind. Here he took on the look of a typical recluse, letting his hair and his beard grow so long that people eventually began to refer to him with the nickname, "Hairy John", that was to stay with him the rest of his life.

But gradually his grief over his wife's suicide decreased to a point where he once again longed for female companionship. Local folk tales say that he finally did find a suitable companion to share his lonely lifestyle, but it seems little is known about her, other than that her name may have been Twila Montray and she may have been the offspring of an Indian woman and a white man. In any case, it would appear that John and his female companion found some happiness, at least for a while, there in their little mountain retreat. However Voneida's life seems to have been destined to be plagued by tragedy.

GHOSTS OF PENN'S WOODS

Tragic events led him to his peaceful existence in the Woodward Narrows, and it was to be violence that ended it.

It's not clear why it happened. Perhaps the little hermit made some enemies because of the way he lived or because of the way he always frightened local children. On the other hand maybe a few local miscreants were convinced that there was a horde of cash hidden in the hermit's cabin. Whatever the case may be, John Voneida apparently became a marked man in the eyes of a few jaded individuals who regarded the small thin recluse as easy prey and set upon him and his woman friend one day, beating them both so badly that they died from the injuries.

There is, of course, the idea, typical in ghost tales throughout the world, that victims of violent deaths come back to haunt the scenes of their demise. But in this case the local tales say that John had always expressed a wish that his spirit would find a home in a beech tree when he died, and that this is where it found its peace. Although that seems more like a fairy tale to us today, there is yet another tale that claims that Twila Montray's spirit haunts the Narrows because it wants to be near the beech tree that holds John's spirit. It is her ghost, they say, that can be seen flitting across and along the road on peaceful summer nights when winds are low, the moon is full, and whippoorwills call from the depths of laurel thickets on Winkelblech Mountain; and at least one couple would agree that the tale is a true one.

GHOSTS OF PENN'S WOODS

One fall evening about thirty years ago the young couple was driving through the Woodward Narrows and had an experience that some might say substantiates the Twila Montray ghost story in a convincing way. It was about 9:30 PM, and they remember the night as being clear and beautiful, with no fog to diffuse the car's headlights. Their vehicle was heading west, towards the little village of Woodward, and they had just passed Hairy John's Park about two miles back when suddenly, and seemingly out of nowhere, something strange appeared on the road ahead.

The dense cloud surprised them since it appeared so unexpectedly and because it was in motion. As they got closer they could see that it was moving from left to right, almost as though it was intentionally trying to cross the highway. They couldn't distinctly discern any kind of definitive shape, but the woman's first impression was that whatever it was, it wasn't fog and it was bigger than a deer. But it wasn't moving fast enough, and, since they were traveling too fast to be able to avoid it, they were upon it in a second, thinking at that point that there was a person there and they were about to hit them. It seemed as though time itself momentarily stood still as they passed through the mist, and they both had the distinct sense at that moment that they had hit something solid. The sensation was so distinct and frightening that the young woman grabbed the dashboard and screamed, while her husband instinctively hit the brakes to try to avoid the accident.

However the expected collision never occurred. There was not any kind of thump or bump that would accompany any such accident, but instead the young couple heard a gentle swishing noise similar to the sound a rushing wind would make as it passes through the needles of a pine tree on a cool sunny afternoon in the fall of the year. But then the car stalled. It was not a place where the couple wanted to tarry, but after the car coasted to a stop they decided that the husband should get out and make sure no one had been hurt. A close inspection of the car revealed no damage, and a check of the highway behind them was also equally puzzling since there was nothing there.

It was an unnerving experience for both of them and especially for the young man, who would later recall that as he was walking around the car he felt "creepy" because he couldn't shake off the intense feeling that something was wrong and he couldn't pinpoint the reason why. To this day he still considers the event as one of the weirdest experiences of his life, believing that on that bizarre autumn night near Hairy John's Park he and his wife drove through a ghost.

GHOSTS OF PENN'S WOODS

The sign at Voncida State Forest Park (now Hairy John State Forest Picnic Area) and a view of the Woodward Narrows back in the 1920's.

The sign today at Hairy John State Forest Picnic Area and a view of the place where Hairy John had his cabin in the Woodward Narrows during the nineteenth century.

CORNWALL IRON FURNACE

It's probably safe to say that there are very few people who have not heard of Sherlock Holmes. The great fictional detective was a creation of author Sir Arthur Conan Doyle, and one of Holmes' most famous cases was one that Doyle himself described as "a real creeper". The case in question was the one Doyle titled "The Hound of the Baskervilles", and it has become a classic of the Holmesian canon. What many people do not realize, however, is that Doyle's tale about a hellish pack of hounds has set down roots in Pennsylvania as well.

The Baskerville hounds were said to be a phantom pack that appeared on the bleak moors of the Yorkshire hills when members of the Baskerville family were about to die. It was an old legend that had existed for centuries around the Dartmoor wastelands of England's' West Country, and its roots were grounded in fact. The legend was based on the 17th century life and escapades of Richard Cabell, whose tomb can still be seen in the town of Buckfastleigh.

"Squire" Cabell, it was said, had a passion for hunting as well as for women and strong drinks, and his fame for immorality became widespread. Locals were so convinced that he had sold his soul to the devil that when Cabell died and was laid to rest in the local graveyard in 1677 there were those who claimed that on that very night they witnessed a phantom pack of baying hounds come running across the moor to howl at his tomb. And thereafter it was also thought that every night on the anniversary of his death Cabell's ghost stirred from its resting place so it could lead that same phantom pack over the moors once again. On all other nights it was believed that if the pack were not out hunting on their own they could be seen circling around Cabell's grave as they howled and shrieked in the most hideous fashion.

Eventually, in order to "lay" Cabell's ghost once and for all and to keep it from escaping, the townspeople walled up the tomb and placed a large stone slab over the grave itself. Their efforts may have quieted their ghost, but a version of its story seems to have found its way to Pennsylvania; at least that's what visitors to Cornwall Iron Furnace in Lebanon County may think once they hear the odd tale that was once told here.

Described as "a site of transcendent significance" by the Smithsonian Institution, the only surviving intact charcoal cold blast furnace in the western hemisphere is now part of an area that is designated as a National Historic Landmark District. In operation from 1742 to 1883, the furnace supplied war materials for both the Revolutionary as well as the Civil Wars, and with that kind of longevity it's not surprising that it has accumulated some interesting stories over the years, including the one about its phantom pack.

When Peter Grubb opened his iron-making operations in 1732, naming it after his hometown of Cornwall in England, he hired Samuel Jacobs as his first iron master. Jacobs, like his English counterpart Cabell, was said to be fond of hunting and kept a fine pack of hunting dogs on site to help him on his excursions for deer, bear, foxes, rabbits, and other local game animals. However, like Cabell, Jacobs too was fond of his whiskey, and often succumbed to its soothing powers. It was an addiction, so claims the Cornwall Furnace tale that led to Jacobs' eternal damnation.

The irascible old iron master had a high opinion of himself as well as of his pack of hounds, until one day they let him down. Jacobs had been bragging to some city friends about how his pack could always be relied upon to tree any game they scented, and one day when those friends told him to "put his money where his mouth was", Jacobs agreed to the wager. But from the outset the pack seemed to hold back; did not exhibit their usual enthusiasm for the hunt. It was the same all day, and by the end of the day the tired and embarrassed host vowed his revenge, while turning to his whisky for comfort.

By the time darkness fell, the besotted iron master had drunk himself into a fury, and it was at the height of that fury that he declared that he would throw each one of his "miserable" dogs into his fiery furnace. It was said that the howls of the beasts could be heard over the roar of the blast furnace as each dog met its horrible end. But Jacobs' end was horrible as well, for according to the tale the dogs came back; returned as a phantom pack to take Jacobs' spirit straight to hell on the day he died. And there are those who say that same pack can be heard now and again as they wander the hills surrounding the ancient furnace.

I tried to confirm the tale; tried to talk to someone who had heard the phantom pack, but no one at the furnace that day had ever talked to anyone who claimed to have done so. On the other hand they told me that nearby there was an old stagecoach stop, just down the road, that had the reputation for being one of the most haunted places in the state. It was from that tip that I ended up at the Farmers Hope Inn in Lebanon County.

We arrived at the Inn late one evening several weeks later, and the orange glow of the setting sun gave the historic stone building a decidedly haunted look. Or maybe that was a feeling inspired by the fact that we had rented a room in the nineteenth-century stagecoach stop in order to attend one of the owners' Paranormal Nights. The venue has proven to be a popular attraction in recent years since it affords guests a chance to tour the Inn's haunted rooms while hearing tales about the ghosts that inhabit them. There is also usually a medium on hand to give readings for those wishing to make contacts with relatives who have "crossed over" to the other side, and on the night we were there the dimly-lit dining room was packed with people who found both the tour and the readings to be as intriguing as they had hoped.

As we went from room to room and then down into the dark and uninviting basement, we learned that the guest rooms are named after the Inn's ghosts and that there are at least six, if not more, spirits that reputedly haunt the place. The apparitions, we were told, are not only of men, but of women and children as well, and their origins span over a century, beginning in the 1830's and ending in the 1940's. Moreover we realized that most all of their stories are unpleasant ones; accounts without happy endings since the unsettled specters seemingly have yet to find eternal rest.

Why that would be true in the case of the most recent haunting is not clear, but sightings of Stanley Peiffer, owner of what he then called the Stagecoach Inn during the late 1940's, have persisted since his death. It seems Stanley likes to stand on the outside porch beside the front door to greet guests coming into the place, or at least that's what those attuned to such things claim, and he's also been seen in other parts of the Inn at times; a fact which has led the current owners to dub him as the Inn's "guardian spirit" and name their Room 7 after him. Apparently Stanley loved his establishment so much when he was flesh and blood that he enjoys coming back for a visit himself now and then. However, that would not be true in the case of the Inn's other ghosts, which, it appears, seem bound to the place for one tragic reason or another.

One such spirit is that of the ghost who haunts Room 1; the room of the Unknown Soldier. It's believed that there are imprinted images of soldiers from both the Revolutionary War and the Civil War that unexpectedly surface once in a while inside the Inn, but the most vivid and detailed image is that of a Confederate soldier who reportedly died here after receiving a mortal wound during the battle at Gettysburg or at some other nearby skirmish. His body, some say, was buried in the basement of the place because either the ground outside was frozen too hard for burial or because the man was not from the area. Then too, it may have been necessary to keep the burial a secret because otherwise the family would have been labeled as southern sympathizers if neighbors had found out they had been harboring a Confederate soldier. In any case, how he would have gotten here is not clear, nor is his name known, but those who have seen his spirit say he lies in agony on a bed, writhing in pain and frequently passing out due to his partially severed leg which was almost torn apart by a cannon ball. Those who can see him also say that when they do so they are also overwhelmed by a strong and pungent odor of ether or other strong chemicals used as pain relievers during that time period. But, say those same sensitives, the soldier's cries do not go unanswered.

Those who have seen him also claim to have seen the spirit of the former maid who ministers to the mortally wounded warrior. She appears to be locked in the same time warp as the man she so faithfully attends, and she's been seen walking up and down the steps leading to the soldier's room, pausing now and then at the hall closet to remove articles of fresh linen that she uses to care for her patient. Apparently caught in a time "loop" she repeats this action over and over again, with the only variation being an occasional trip to wash soiled linen in an outside well, which was recently uncovered by the Inn's owners and which can be seen there today. Her distinguishing feature is her white dress with a red border of what appear to be red roses around the bottom. The red "decorations", on the other hand, are thought by some to be blood stains from the gruesome task she endlessly performs.

Since it was built in 1812, the Inn has had almost two-hundred years to attract its ghosts, and in addition to those of its soldiers, the Inn also claims to be home to the spirit of a ten or eleven year old boy whose name has been assigned to Room 3. Charles' Room is dedicated to the son of an early stagecoach driver who transported passengers through here during the late 1800's. Little Charles was an apprentice, and his father was training him for a career as a stagecoach driver. It seemed like a natural fit since Charles loved to drive the stage and tend to its horses and customers alike. But one year the young lad was beset by a bad cough, which worsened as time went on and the balmy breezes of summer turned into the harsh cold blasts of winter.

Doctors eventually diagnosed the problem as "consumption", which physicians now refer to as pulmonary tuberculosis. The illness proved to be a scourge to all rural Pennsylvanians in the 1800's and early 1900's, and one day after Charles and his father arrived at the Inn, the little lad could go no further. They placed him in the room which bears his name, and two days later he died there. His emaciated body was buried under the supple branches of the willow tree that still stands in back of the stagecoach stop he knew so well. It's said that to this day Charles' spirit loves to rock in the rocking chair in the room named after him, and there have been guests who have seen the chair seemingly rocking on its own. Others have reported seeing the boy's ghost cavorting under the willow and playing with its branches.

There are three other ghosts that haunt the old Inn and which predate the others. Rooms 2, 4, and 5 are named after them, and their origins, it's thought, date back to the 1830's when the place was still under the management of John Koch, its original owner.

Koch would be sued for sexual harassment today, but back then he could get away with such things, and his barmaids were often subjected to his unwelcome advances when he became drunk from drinking too much of his own beer. One young lady in particular seemed to attract him more than others, and late one night the drunken Koch began to chase her through the dining room of the Inn. Nineteen year old Sarah did not think she had any other choice but to submit to him in order to keep her job, and as a result became pregnant by the lecherous innkeeper. Nine months later she gave birth to her daughter Elizabeth, and shortly after that she died from childbirth complications.

The young child was raised by the staff at the Inn, who admired her playful spirit and her youthful beauty. By the time she reached age seven Elizabeth's eyes were large and beautiful, her skin was fair and unblemished, and her hair was long and brown. She became much admired by staff and patrons alike, but her father would never publicly acknowledge her as his child and he kept her under a tight rein. Full of energy, Elizabeth loved to chase butterflies in the garden and she also loved to mingle with her father's customers as they came in at night. Koch, on the other hand, called her a "little pest" if she seemed to be making a nuisance of herself, and, as punishment, would lock her in the basement. Then one night Koch got drunk once again, and in his inebriated condition decided that Elizabeth was bothering the customers more than usual. In a drunken rage he grabbed her arm and threw her down the cellar stairs. The landing proved to be a hard one, and several days later the little girl died from her internal injuries.

Given such a traumatic series of events it's no wonder that the spirits of John Koch, Sarah, and the young Elizabeth still haunt the place where their fates became intertwined. Guests have reported hearing the sound of a young girl laughing and giggling in the garden and have seen her image as she runs along chasing butterflies. Others say they've seen the ghost of a young barmaid wearing a blue dress with white apron and bonnet running from the barroom to the front dining area of the Inn as she's chased by the apparition of what appears to be an elderly man. It is, they believe, the spirits of John Koch and Sarah, which seem destined to continually repeat their earthly actions until they are able to reach a spiritual plateau where they can achieve some measure of peace at last.

Koch may, however, find that to be more difficult than Sarah. He is, say the psychics who claim to be able to communicate with him, reluctant to have his story told, whereas Sarah wants the truth to come out. That may be why Koch's spirit is the more restless of the two; why his likeness suddenly and inexplicably appeared on a window pane in the dining room in 2008. The profile was amazing and looked like a photograph had been etched into the glass. It drew comments from customers for some time until one day it disappeared as suddenly and as mysteriously as it had appeared. To this day the Inn's owners have no explanation for it, but instead chalk it up to just another psychic event in their haunted inn.

Cornwall Furnace and the opening to its fiery pit

GHOSTS OF PENN'S WOODS

Farmers Hope Inn

GHOSTS OF PENN'S WOODS

The haunted dining room at Farmers Hope Inn